Elfrida

ABOUT THE AUTHOR

Elizabeth Norton gained her first degree from the University of Cambridge and her Masters from the University of Oxford. She is the author of ten books on the Tudors. She lives in London.

PRAISE FOR ELIZABETH NORTON

Catherine Parr

'Scintillating... Norton cuts an admirably clear path through tangled Tudor intrigues'

JENNY UGLOW, *THE FINANCIAL TIMES*

'Eminently readable... Norton's strength is in her use of original sources'

SARAH GRISTWOOD, *BBC HISTORY MAGAZINE*

Bessie Blount

'Secret of the queen that Britain "lost"' *THE SUN*

'A lucid, readable, intelligent account of the life of a woman who might have been queen'

THE GOOD BOOK GUIDE

Anne Boleyn: In Her Own Words & the Words of Those

Who Knew Her

'A very useful compilation of source material on Anne Boleyn... a well produced book'

ALISON WEIR

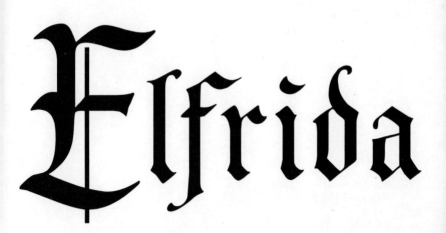

Elfrida

The First Crowned
Queen of England

ELIZABETH
NORTON

AMBERLEY

First published 2013

This edition first published 2014

Amberley Publishing
The Hill, Stroud
Gloucestershire, GL5 4EP

www.amberley-books.com

ISBN 978 1 4456 3765 5 (paperback)
ISBN 978 1 4456 1492 2 (ebook)

British Library Cataloguing in Publication Data.
A catalogue record for this book is available from the British Library.

Printed in the UK.

Contents

I

ELFRIDA'S EARLY LIFE

English history has produced many great and memorable queens, some with less than wholesome reputations. None can be said to have a reputation as black as the very first woman to be crowned as queen of all England: the archetypal wicked stepmother, Queen Elfrida.

Today Elfrida is remembered only for the murder of her stepson, King Edward the Martyr, which cleared the way for her son, Ethelred, to take the crown. The extent of her involvement (if any) is debatable, but mud sticks. The question is, how did a religious and gifted woman, who rose from obscurity to become Queen of England, come to be vilified within only a few short decades of her death? Along with her husband and a number of prominent churchmen, Elfrida ushered in one of the greatest religious reforms England has ever known. She and Edgar presided over a time of great cultural accomplishments and peace. How did the drama of the life of one of the most vivid and powerful women of her time come to be defined by one dark day in March 978? And just who was Queen Elfrida?

The girl who was born in the mid-940s would not have called herself Elfrida. Following the Norman Conquest in 1066 English parents began, increasingly, to choose Norman first names for their children, abandoning more traditional Anglo-Saxon choices. In 1002, when Emma of Normandy arrived to marry the English king, she was asked to change her name to the very popular 'Aelfgifu', as the name Emma was unheard of in England: to modern ears, it is Aelfgifu that is outlandish. Elfrida is the Latin form of the Old English name Aelfthryth. It is this that was Elfrida's true name but, to modern eyes, Elfrida is clearer and easier to read. 'Aelfthryth', which should be spelled with the ash symbol of the joined letters 'ae', is not the only name difficult to modern readers. For ease, the modern form of names will be used here, such as 'Edgar' instead of 'Eadgar'. The ash symbol will also generally be given as a single 'E', with 'Aethelred' becoming 'Ethelred', for example. Exceptions to this are where such names are more usually spelled with an 'A' so 'Aethelstan' becomes 'Athelstan' and 'Aelfred' 'Alfred'. While not strictly speaking correct, this will make matters clearer. Aelfthryth or Elfrida was a popular name with royal connections; daughters of King Offa of Mercia and Alfred the Great both bore the name.[1]

Elfrida's father was a nobleman named Ordgar, who first appears in the records as a witness to a charter of King Eadwig in 958.[2] In the highly stratified Anglo-Saxon society, he was a thegn, which was the second rank of society, below ealdormen but well above ceorls and the slave class.[3] The Norman historian Gaimar, writing in the early twelfth century, had heard that Ordgar was immensely wealthy, with land in every settlement from Exeter in Devon to Frome in Somerset, a distance of over 70 miles.[4] Elfrida's family also had an association with Tavistock, which is 30 miles west of Exeter. Even allowing for exaggeration, Ordgar's landholdings appear to have been significant.

The family's wealth can also be seen in the grandeur of Tavistock Abbey, which was founded by Elfrida's brother, Ordulf, during the reign of King Edgar. When the traveller William of Worcester visited the abbey in the late fifteenth century, he found a large building, with a substantial church and a lady chapel, nave and choirs.[5] A twelfth-century source claims that Ordgar was the son of an ealdorman, the highest rank in the Anglo-Saxon nobility.[6] Such a position was not hereditary and, for most of Elfrida's early life, Ordgar was a wealthy thegn. His absence from sources earlier than 958 suggests that he was rarely at court, instead remaining within his own sphere of interest in the West Country.

Elfrida's mother died long before her daughter's marriage.[7] She was of royal descent but her name and family are unclear.[8] She is perhaps the Eadgifu referred to as the wife of Ordgar in the Leofric Missal, but this may refer to an eleventh-century Ordgar instead.[9] Much of the tenth-century nobility was descended from King Ethelred I, the elder brother of King Alfred, and this is a probable lineage for Elfrida's mother.[10] She was evidently remembered fondly by her son, Ordulf, as, many years after her death when he founded Tavistock Abbey, he arranged for his mother and a deceased brother to be buried within the church there.[11] This brother may have been the Elfsige for whose soul Ordulf freed a slave from one of his estates in Cornwall soon after his father's death.[12] He probably survived until adulthood at least, since his brother went to the trouble of exhuming him. His nephew, King Ethelred, referred to Tavistock Abbey, stating that Ordulf's 'mother and brother, to wit my Grandmother and Uncle, and others the ancestors of our posterity are honourably buried'.[13]

With the exception of this brother, Ordulf is Elfrida's only known sibling. A document in the cartulary of Wherwell Abbey that refers to a brother of Elfrida's named Alfred as the abbey's founder is almost certainly an error, based on a mistake in the copying of the name 'Alfreda' or Elfrida, the house's true foundress.[14] It appears that his father's dynastic hopes were centred on Ordulf, with a later Ordgar and Ordulf from the West Country appearing in documents from the eleventh century suggested as his descendants.[15] If this assumption is correct then Ordgar's dynastic hopes were met for a time, with a nobleman named Ordulf one of the greatest landowners in Devon in 1066.[16] This position could not last, however, and, by the time of the Domesday Book in 1086, fifteen of Ordgar's twenty manors had been taken from his control.

Elfrida, as the family's only daughter, was a great favourite of her father and was used to getting her own way. According to Gaimar, 'what his daughter counselled him, what she did or what she commanded to do, no man was found who dared dissuade him from'.[17] Few details of Elfrida's early life survive, although she is known to have lived in Devon.[18] Traditionally her father, Ordgar, was supposed to have lived at Tavistock, with the site of his house still pointed out to interested visitors early in the nineteenth century.[19] Unfortunately this tradition was based on the erroneous assumption that he was the founder of the abbey, but, given the family's association with the place, it may have an element of truth.

The family also spent time on their other estates. Parts of Devon and Cornwall had only been incorporated into the West Saxon kingdom in the ninth century and Elfrida would have been aware of the surviving British culture in the area. A number of slave manumissions, which record a landowner freeing slaves for pious reasons, were preserved at Exeter Cathedral. These include manumissions relating to Elfrida's family, such as a document in which either her father, or the later Ordgar, recorded that he had freed ten slaves 'at Bradstone, where he lay sick'.[20] The names of the individual slaves are a mixture of Anglo-Saxon and British names, suggesting that, culturally, Ordgar's estates were mixed.[21]

Slaves were also employed as household servants, with surviving Wills from the period referring to them as women-weavers and seamstresses, for example, all of whom Elfrida would have come into daily contact with.[22] An early eleventh-century Will confirmed the position of many servants, with the testator freeing all her men 'in the household, and on the estate' for the good of her soul.[23]

Close bonds could be formed between a mistress and a household slave: the tenth-century Will of Wynflaed, for example, provided for a slave called Wulfflaed to be freed, but only on the proviso that she served her mistress's daughter and granddaughter. Further manumissions made by an Eadgifu, for the benefit of Ordgar, may relate to Elfrida's mother and suggest that her father suffered ill health during her childhood, requiring his wife to take action on behalf of his soul. Elfrida's brother, Ordulf, freed a woman named 'Gluiucen' in Cornwall not long after their father's death, further evidence of the family's familiarity with Britons.[24] Given that these slaves were often used for household service, it is likely that Elfrida was familiar with British customs from her childhood, alongside the Anglo-Saxon traditions into which she was raised. She spent much time with her father, who taught her chess in order to allow the pair to play together.[25]

Under Anglo-Saxon law, a distinction was made between a man's 'folk lands', which were inherited automatically by his eldest son, and his 'book lands', which were acquired property and which they were free to dispose of as they wished. Although she was not her father's heir, it was well known during her youth that her father's favour meant that she would inherit considerable wealth and that he would provide her with a rich dowry.[26]

The date or location of Elfrida's birth is not recorded, although it was probably in the mid-940s and in Devon. While her mother lived, she would have supervised her daughter's infancy and early education. Alternatively, she may have been fostered with a local family.

No specific details of Elfrida's education survive. Her brother, Ordulf, may have understood Latin, since he commissioned a stone tablet containing verse in that language at his foundation of Tavistock Abbey.[27] It has also been suggested by one recent historian that he 'had some pretensions to learning and a more general interest in theological matters' than the majority of his contemporaries.[28] Ordulf was probably of a similar age to Elfrida. Although he did not begin to attend court and attest charters until 975, four years after his father's death, he is known to have been active in Devon and Conwall at least a few years before that date, with the date of his foundation suggested as 974.[29] He also carried out a manumission in Cornwall very soon after his father's death, suggesting some continuation of authority there. Elfrida herself later jointly commissioned a translation of the Rule of St Benedict into English with her husband King Edgar. However, given that this was part of the couple's attempts to promulgate the Rule throughout England, it need not necessarily suggest that they were ignorant of the language themselves. King Edgar's great-grandfather, Alfred the Great, had lamented the lack of Latin learning in England at the end of the ninth century and took efforts to improve the situation, and so a grounding in the language is not impossible, although it is doubtful that a woman who was intended for marriage rather than the Church would have received such an education.

While it is doubtful that Elfrida received a grounding in Latin, even in the event that her brother did, it is likely that she would have shared many of his tutors since the education of high-status girls in Anglo-Saxon England was encouraged. An example of a brother and sister receiving the same education is given by the ninth-century writer Asser, in his biography of his patron, King Alfred. According to Asser, two of Alfred's children, Edward and Elfrida,

> were at all times fostered at the royal court under the solicitous care of tutors and nurses, and indeed with the great love of all; and to the present day they continue to behave with humility, friendliness and gentleness to all compatriots and foreigners, and with great obedience to their father. Nor, amid the other pursuits of this present life which are appropriate to the nobility, are these two allowed to live idly and indifferently, with no liberal education, for they have attentively learned the Psalms, and books in English, and especially English poems, and they very frequently make use of books.[30]

No distinction was made between the education of the future king, Edward, and his sister, Elfrida's own namesake. While this example is from the highest level of society, it is clear that noblemen's daughters were also educated. The ninth-century noblewoman Osburh, who was the daughter of King Ethelwulf's butler[31] and later married her father's master, possessed a book of English poetry, which she read from and encouraged her sons to learn to read themselves.[32] Edith, the daughter of the eleventh-century ealdorman Godwin, was educated at the nunnery of Wilton, leaving her schoolroom fluent in Irish, French and Danish and skilled in Latin and English verse.[33] Edith, who became the wife of Edward the Confessor, was renowned for her learning and should be considered as an extreme example of the education of women.[34] However, examples such as hers make it clear that noblewomen were very likely to be educated in the late Anglo-Saxon period. Elfrida's predecessor as Edgar's wife, Wulfthryth, certainly was.

Based on this, it can be reasonably assumed that Elfrida could at least read and write in her own language, and would have been familiar with some works of contemporary literature. She certainly later showed herself well versed in contemporary religious ideas, suggesting a thorough education. According to one later medieval account, even before she was queen men 'spoke of her wit, and that which she understood; that she was both fair and wise'.[35] She was aware of her intelligence, being considered to be 'of free courage in speaking' on occasion, something that perhaps echoes the criticism of the later, well-educated queen Edith Godwin, that she lacked humility.

The main aim of Elfrida's childhood was to equip her for her future as a nobleman's wife. Elfrida was famed for her beauty in her home county of Devon, with news of her appearance reaching the king's court.[36] In common with a number of Anglo-Saxon noblewomen, she acquired a nickname in her youth, being known as Elfrida the Fair.[37] She stood out among the other noblewomen of her time and, although no description of her survives, it is claimed in stories surrounding her that both her husbands fell in love with her at first sight.

Elfrida was recorded as having a queenly appearance and it is possible that this was in part due to being unusually tall. Her brother, Ordulf, was 'as big as a giant and immensely strong', with the twelfth-century historian, William of Malmesbury, recording an anecdote in his history to illustrate this. According to William, Ordulf

> was journeying to Exeter with his kinsman, King Edgar. When they jumped down from their horses at the town gates, they found the entrance closed with bars on the outside and locked on the inside. It so happened that the doorkeeper had not known about their arrival, for they were riding at a time of internal peace, and he had gone far away so Eadwulf [Ordulf] took hold of the bars in both hands and with seemingly little effort threw them to the ground in pieces, at the same time tearing part of the wall as well. Now that his blood was up, with a savage gnashing of his teeth he gave a second proof of his manliness. Weakening the doors with his kicking, he broke away their double hinges so fiercely that he destroyed their material as well. Everyone else applauded, but the king made light of the matter and jokingly attributed it to diabolical strength, not human powers.[38]

During the eighteenth century the Chapter House at Tavistock Abbey was demolished, and two thigh bones were found inside a stone sarcophagus.[39] In the early twentieth century these were examined by an osteologist, who considered that they were ancient and belonged to two men, both of whom were extremely tall. The larger of the two bones was considered to fulfil 'all that one could expect of the great Earl Ordulf, for the man of whose frame it formed part, must have been of extraordinary strength and stature. He was very old at the time of his death, but in his prime must have stood nearly 7 feet high, so that the story of striding across rivers is not incredible.'[40] The chapter house of a monastery, which would often be used for burials of high-status individuals, is a plausible place for the founder, Elfrida's brother Ordulf, to have been buried and the analysis of the deceased's age and height do support the identification. William of Malmesbury, who erroneously claimed that Elfrida's father was buried at Tavistock Abbey, may have meant the later Ordgar, the son or grandson of Ordulf. If so, he is a possible candidate for the second thigh bone.[41] An 'Elfgar the Tall', who held manors at Domesday connected to the family, has also been suggested as a descendant of Elfrida's family, again suggesting that unusually high stature was a family trait.[42] Elfrida certainly shared the robust health and longevity of the rest of her family. Her father, Ordgar, survived until 971, when he was at least in his fifties. Elfrida herself was approaching sixty at her death, while her brother was still alive in 1008, making him very elderly for the time. Elfrida's own son, Ethelred II, was one of the longest-reigning of any Anglo-Saxon king. While the *Liber Eliensis* referred to Elfrida in her old age as 'one little woman', this seems more likely to refer to her status as a woman alone in relation to the incident described rather than an attempt to actually describe her appearance.[43]

Elfrida stood out, both for her beauty and her social position. It is therefore no surprise that she was able to attract a husband from the highest level of the English nobility.

2

FIRST MARRIAGE

Elfrida's early life would have prepared her to marry once she was old enough and to run her own household. She always knew that her future lay in marriage: the Old English word for woman is, literally, 'wife' and marriage was seen as the usual state for women.[1] The only other accepted option was the life of a nun, something which, before the religious reform of the tenth century in which Elfrida was involved, would have been difficult to achieve. Women were not completely powerless in the arrangements made for their marriages, however. As the wife of a nobleman, Elfrida could expect a valuable marriage gift from her husband, which was often land, and which would be under her personal control.[2] This was designed to give her independence during her widowhood and, while no evidence of Elfrida's marriage gift survives, the status of her bridegroom and the prestige of her father suggest that it was substantial.

The man chosen to be Elfrida's husband was Ethelwold, the eldest son of Athelstan, Ealdorman of East Anglia. This Athelstan was prominent through much of the middle part of the tenth century, to the extent that he was nicknamed '"Half-King", since he was a man of such authority that he was said to maintain the kingdom and its rule with his advice to the king'.[3] It has been estimated that, at the height of his career, he ruled an area the size of Normandy, with very little royal interference.[4] He was particularly influential during the reign of King Edgar's father, King Edmund, who was young when he came to the throne. The Half-King has, in fact, been likened to a regent, and while this might be a slight exaggeration, there is no doubt that he was Edmund's most trusted advisor, with his wife being entrusted with the upbringing of Edgar himself following the early death of his mother. The Half-King was the second of four sons born to Ethelfrith, an ealdorman with authority in Mercia but with considerable landholdings in Somerset and Devon. Athelstan Half-King was married to a woman named Elfwynn, who 'had a distinguished lineage' and was a member of a prominent Huntingdonshire family.[5] The couple had four sons: Ethelwold, Elfwold, Ethelsige and Ethelwine.

The family of Athelstan Half-King were the wealthiest and most prominent in England at the time of Elfrida's marriage. The Half-King's brother, Elfstan, who appears to have succeeded to his father's ealdordom, is known to have been close to King Athelstan, travelling north with the court to Northampton in 934 where he witnessed a royal charter.[6] He probably died that summer during the king's Scottish campaign.

The Will of an earlier Ealdorman Ethelwold, who was the brother of the Half-King and for whom Elfrida's husband was named, survives, showing something of the family's prestige and interests. This Ethelwold was prominent at court between 931 and 946. He was pious and gave land at Wiley to the episcopal see of Winchester 'for the provision of clothing, so that they may remember me in their prayers, as I believe that they will'.[7] Ealdorman Ethelwold also made land bequests to his two living brothers, Eadric and Athelstan, both of whom were ealdormen, as well as gifts to a number of nephews. As a wealthy man he was liable for a substantial heriot (a type of death duty) to the king of 'four swords, four spears, four shields, four bracelets, two worth 120 mancuses, and two worth 8 mancuses, four horses and two silver cups'.

The prestige of Elfrida's father-in-law, the most prominent of the brothers, was also substantial. At some point before 931, for example, he was able to command a prominent place at a meeting otherwise made up of bishops and abbots who witnessed a grant of land made by him of land to Abingdon Abbey.[8] This shows an early interest in monasticism and is in line with the Half-King's reputation as a benefactor of religious reform. He was also able to ensure that his grant to the abbey was secure even after his death, recording in a charter that

> Archbishop Wulfhelm and all the bishops and abbots who were there assembled excommunicated from Christ and from all the fellowship of Christ and from the whole of Christendom anyone who should ever undo this grant or reduce this estate in pasture of in boundary. He shall be cut off and hurled into the abyss of hell for ever without end. And all the people who stood by said, 'so be it, Amen, Amen'.

Elfrida's father-in-law was a man used to getting his own way and was not prepared to tolerate any opposition. He did, however, fall foul of King Eadwig, early in his reign, with the elderly Half-King retiring to Glastonbury as a monk in 956. This retirement may well have been negotiated with the king, as his eldest son, Ethelwold, immediately succeeded to his ealdordom, soon after marrying

Elfrida.[9] He had first begun to appear at court in 956, when he started to witness royal charters, first as a thegn and then, later in the year, as ealdorman, suggesting that he had been somewhat hurriedly brought to court by a father anxious to retire.[10]

Ethelwold's time as ealdorman was brief, but he was evidently considered to be successful, holding it 'with great authority'.[11] The second brother, Elfwold, was equally prominent, being described by a contemporary as being 'exalted with such great authority, that he ever disdained to become an ealdorman'.[12] He was apparently 'tall in stature, courteous in speech, worthy in appearance', although his features could take on 'a fiery expression' when the occasion demanded.[13] The third brother, Ethelsige, did become an ealdorman, although it was the youngest, Ethelwine, who was the most prominent of the four, ruling as ealdorman of East Anglia for thirty years. Ethelwine was, apparently, a particularly fine specimen of a man, being described by one contemporary as being 'excellent in body and bearing', 'possessed of urbane eloquence' and 'attractive in his appearance and in all his limbs'.[14] No description survives of Ethelwold but he appears to have been equally admired during his short life, being described, with his three brothers, as a 'flower of the nobility'.[15]

No certain details survive surrounding the circumstances of Elfrida's marriage. A fourteenth-century Life of Ethelwold's daughter, Ethelflaed, later claimed that King Edgar arranged his first marriage to a lady who was a close relative of his queen, as a reward for Ethelwold's good service.[16] Although this wife was named as Brihtgifu and the queen was Elfrida herself, as discussed below, it is not impossible that the mother of Ethelflaed was in fact Elfrida, and that the circumstances of this match refer to her own marriage. Edgar's first wife, whom he married while he was King of the Mercians, has been called Ethelflaed, daughter of Ealdorman Ordmaer. The background to this marriage will be considered later but it is possible that Ethelflaed was the daughter of a thegn called Ordmaer who was recorded in the *Liber Eliensis* as entering into an agreement with Athelstan Half-King to exchange his lands in Hatfield in Hertfordshire for lands of the Half-King in Somerset.[17] The fact that Ordmaer required lands in the West Country, coupled with the similarity of the first element of his name with Elfrida's father, Ordgar, does open up the possibility that the two men were related, particularly since the men in Elfrida's family were commonly given names beginning with 'Ord'.[18] This is also plausible given the fact that Queen Ethelflaed's son, Edward the Martyr, was raised by Bishop Sideman at Exeter, a location well within the sphere of influence of Elfrida's father and his family.[19] It is therefore not at all impossible that the only wife of Ethelwold was Elfrida, who was a kinswoman of the queen, Ethelflaed, and that the marriage was arranged by the king, something that would place the marriage in around 958 when Edgar became King of the Mercians.

Other stories surrounding the marriage also suggest that Edgar was involved in arranging it. Alternatively, it has been suggested that as the Half-King began to lose influence at court during the regin of Edgar's brother, Eadwig, he hurriedly brought his eldest son, who was then in his early twenties, to court to marry the daughter of the wealthy Ordgar.[20] According to this analysis, the Half-King was then able to negotiate his retirement with Eadwig, with the king allowing Ethelwold to take the family's West Country estates. A match between Elfrida and Ethelwold certainly made sense territorially and, while Ethelwold's family had begun to turn their sphere of influence towards East Anglia by the mid-tenth century, they still held hereditary lands in Somerset and Devon, close to Ordgar's own: it is not impossible that Elfrida and Ethelwold were already known to each other, as their respective fathers' households may, on occasion, have been neighbours. This would not have been a regular occurrence, however, since the Half-King's interests by the 950s were largely in East Anglia and his main residence was situated on his wife's lands in the Huntingdonshire fens.[21] Although both were active at court to a certain extent during the reign of King Eadwig, they do not attest any surviving charters together, suggesting that any acquaintance was not through royal attendance.

However the marriage came to be arranged, it probably occurred between 956 and 958, when Elfrida would have been in her teens and Ethelwold his early twenties. Little is recorded of Ethelwold's time in office, although he supported Edgar when he became King of the Mercians in 958, abandoning his loyalty to King Eadwig. He was evidently not particularly well regarded at court, generally witnessing only as the fourth of five ealdormen during this period.[22] Gaimar's claim that, towards the end of his life, after Edgar had succeeded to the entire country, Ethelwold was appointed to rule York and southern Northumbria, is considered plausible by historians.[23] Perhaps he had proved his abilities to the king: something that would suggest that he and his wife were often in the king's presence.

Once the match had been agreed, a marriage agreement would have been entered into by both Ethelwold and Elfrida's family. In Anglo-Saxon England, marriages were seen as the concern of the bride's family and, although the bride was allowed a certain amount of autonomy in the choice of husband, the ultimate power lay with her father and other male kin. This can clearly be seen in a number of examples from the Anglo-Saxon period. For example, Elfrida's predecessor as queen, Judith, was the daughter of the Frankish king Charles the Bald, and was successively the wife of King Ethelwulf of Wessex and his son, King Ethelbald; she was then placed in a nunnery by her father following her second widowhood. She was unhappy with this choice and quickly eloped from her convent with Count Baldwin of Flanders, who was described in a contemporary source as having 'stolen away Charles's daughter and married her', something that demonstrates clearly the prevailing view that a daughter was her father's to bestow.[24]

Several marriage agreements from Elfrida's time survive and show that marriage was essentially approached like a business agreement. In the early eleventh century, that made for a match between a certain Wulfric and Archbishop Wulfstan's sister, a couple who were of similar rank to Ethelwold and Elfrida, provided that the groom was to give his wife land in four estates, as well as fifty mancuses of gold, thirty men and thirty horses.[25] Another surviving Anglo-Saxon marriage agreement contains similar terms, with the bride receiving 150 acres of land, thirty oxen, twenty cows, ten horses and ten slaves.[26] Both dowers would have ensured that the bride was a wealthy woman during her widowhood, something that Elfrida would also have expected. She was certainly left wealthy and independent enough to settle land that had previously belonged to her first husband on Romsey nunnery after his death, as well as assuming financial authority for the upbringing of his daughter.

There are, in fact, two medieval accounts of Elfrida's first marriage, provided by the writers William of Malmesbury and Geoffrey Gaimar. Gaimar, who was probably Norman in origin, wrote his history of England in the first half of the twelfth century, although he frequently made use of the Anglo-Saxon Chronicle and claimed to use an earlier source in relation to the details he gave for Elfrida's first marriage. According to Gaimar, the young Elfrida was living in Devon with her father when reports of her beauty reached the ears of King Edgar.[27] Ordgar was used to receiving visitors from court and Elfrida was involved in welcoming them, ensuring that 'the courtiers who saw her spoke much of her beauty'. Edgar heard this and, according to Gaimar, declared,

> Although here I am a king,
> And she is daughter of a thane,
> I see no difference.
> Her father was an earl's son,
> Her mother sprang from noble kings,
> She is of high birth enough,
> I can take her without shame.

Having resolved to marry Elfrida if she proved worthy, Edgar sent for his friend, Ethelwold, to declare to him that he was in love with Ordgar's daughter and to request that his friend go to her to confirm that she was as beautiful as everyone claimed. Thus commanded, Ethelwold went straight to Devon where he greeted Elfrida on behalf of the king. He spent a day in her company, while she played chess with her father, and fell in love with her. According to Gaimar's version, Ethelwold then hatched a plot to keep Elfrida for himself, informing the king that 'she was not so fair' and going so far as to claim that she 'was misshapen, ugly, and dark', before winning permission from the king to marry her himself, ostensibly only out of desire for her wealth. He then travelled back to Devon where he was welcomed as a son-in-law by Ordgar who, along with Elfrida, was entirely unaware of the king's earlier interest. William of Malmesbury, who also wrote early in the twelfth century, told a similar version of the marriage, stating that Ethelwold informed the king that his bride 'was a girl of vulgar and common-place appearance'.[28]

Both accounts claim that Elfrida was, at first, unaware of the king's interest. According to Gaimar, her husband finally informed her that she might have been a queen after their marriage:

> In this country [Devon] he tarried so long,
> That the lady was pregnant with a son.
> But the fair lady, if she could
> Would never have been pregnant by Ethelwold.
> She did not love him. It had been told her
> How the king had been deceived,
> He himself, all indiscreetly
> Had discovered this to Aelfthryth [Elfrida].
> At the right time the infant was born.

Gaimar presents Ethelwold at best as a liar who won her under false pretences, and at worst, potentially as a man who raped an unwilling bride. To compound his treachery, he arranged for Edgar to stand as godfather to the child, something which created a spiritual relationship between the king and the child's mother as though they were brother and sister. According to Gaimar, Edgar attended the christening himself to 'hold this child at the font' while Ethelwold kept Elfrida away and out of sight of the king. Both accounts make it clear that this state of affairs could not continue indefinitely.

According to William of Malmesbury, Edgar continued to hear reports of Elfrida's beauty and grew suspicious; 'returning him deceit for deceit, he showed the earl [Ethelwold] a fair countenance, and, as in a sportive manner, appointed a day when he would visit this far-famed lady'. Gaimar also recorded that Edgar became anxious to see her after realising he had been duped since 'for Aelfthryth he was very pensive'. According to Gaimar, Edgar travelled to Devon, claiming that his purpose was a hunting trip. Ordgar's house was close to the forest and he arrived there to stay, asking Ethelwold where the mother of his godchild was, only to be informed that she was in the upper room. Edgar then insisted on seeing her, where he found her with the ladies of her household:

> He knew Aelfthryth by her beauty,
> And she welcomed the king.
> She was veiled in a wimple.
> The king drew it from her head.
> Then he smiled and looked at her,
> And then kissed his commere.[29]
> From this kiss sprang love.
> Aelfthryth was the flower of the others.
> The king in play and jest
> Raised the fold of her mantle
> Then he saw her figure so slender
> For a little he was amazed by the beauty he saw there.

Just what Ethelwold can have made of the king's actions towards his wife are not recorded by Gaimar, who makes it clear that Elfrida was in no way blameworthy for the king's attraction towards her, instead sitting with him to dine in the hall and kissing him at the end of the evening as custom demanded.

William of Malmesbury's account of the meeting is rather more accusatory towards the future queen, claiming that, when he heard the king would arrive, Ethelwold, 'terrified almost to death', rushed to his wife and begged 'that she would administer to his safety by attiring herself as unbecomingly as possible'. Elfrida, however, angry with her husband, refused, proceeding 'to adorn herself at the mirror, and to omit nothing which could stimulate the desire of a young and powerful man'. Both accounts are equally certain that Edgar fell in love with Elfrida at first sight and resolved to have her by any means. In Gaimar, this meant that the king, after a visit of eight days, moved his court to Salisbury, where he summoned Ethelwold and ordered him to travel to York to rule the land north of the Humber. On the road, he was set upon and killed by a party sent by the king. Alternatively, William of Malmesbury claimed that Edgar invited Ethelwold to Wherwell forest in Hampshire where, 'under pretence of hunting' he 'ran him through with a javelin'.

Both accounts were written well over a century after the events that they described, and must be treated with considerable caution. Given the great differences between the two stories, it appears that they used different sources and that, by the early twelfth century, it was widely considered that Edgar had murdered Elfrida's first husband (perhaps with her connivance) so that he could marry her.[30] Of the two, although William of Malmesbury's is perhaps based on the earlier tradition, Gaimar's seems to be the more plausible. Until the reign of Edgar, Gaimar's *History* was based almost solely on the Anglo-Saxon Chronicle and he is therefore likely to have used similarly early sources for the other elements of his work. Gaimar does not appear to have been aware of William's story, which parallels the Biblical story of Uriah very closely in its emphasis on Elfrida's guilt.[31] William's claim that the murder happened at

Wherwell can also be said to be a later elaboration of the reason behind Elfrida's foundation of a nunnery there in her old age, which was popularly considered to have been carried out as an act of atonement. If Elfrida and Ethelwold married in 956 when Ethelwold first came to prominence, then Edgar was not king, and the 'facts' of their marriage related by the two twelfth-century chroniclers are impossible. However, as already set out, it is not impossible that the match occurred in 958 when Edgar was a king. If this is the case, there may be some small element of the truth in the two accounts, particularly Gaimar's. While Elfrida and Edgar may have become romantically involved during Ethelwold's lifetime, the evidence certainly does not suggest that Ethelwold was murdered.

There are at least three possible locations for Elfrida's household during her marriage. The late tenth-century Life of St Oswald, which was written by a monk of Ramsey in a monastery founded by Ethelwold's brother, claimed that after their marriage, Ethelwold brought Elfrida back to 'his kingdom' (i.e. East Anglia).[32] Gaimar, on the other hand, considered that they lived in Devon in her father's house, with Elfrida continuing to act as hostess for her father when the occasion demanded. It has also been suggested that the couple may have lived in Somerset on the estates that King Eadwig granted to Ethelwold on his arrival as a thegn at court.[33] If the couple did marry in 956 then an initial home in the West Country is likely. After the retirement of Athelstan Half-King, however, the couple must have been predominantly based in East Anglia. Ethelwold's brother, Ealdorman Ethelwine, is known to have lived at Upwood, not far from his foundation of Ramsey Abbey in the fens. Perhaps Elfrida made her first home as a married woman in that area.

Little evidence survives on the relationship between the couple. Both Gaimar and William of Malmesbury suggest that they were unhappy, but these later elaborations must be treated with caution. Although Ethelwold's duties as ealdorman often called for his presence at court, the couple spent enough time together for at least one, and possibly three, children to have been born to them.

Gaimar recorded that Elfrida bore her husband a son. This is probably Leofric who is known to have been a son of Ethelwold's and became an important figure in East-Anglian society. Along with his wife, Leofflaed, Leofric founded a monastery at St Neots between 975 and 984 when he was still a young man.[34] He never achieved the prominence of his father, apparently being content to remain on his own estates, although he did witness a land transaction at his uncle's foundation of Ramsey Abbey in June 987.[35] Leofric was remembered by the monks of Ely as 'a man devoted to God', something that suggests he shared his mother's interest in the religious reform movement.[36] There is no evidence of later contact between Elfrida and her eldest son, in spite of the fact that Leofric must have gained a certain status as the half-brother of the king after 978. Most likely, he remained with his paternal family after his father's death, while Elfrida retained custody of any daughters or stepdaughters. There is no evidence of any estrangement between Elfrida and Ethelwold's family until 975, over a decade after Ethelwold's death, and the decision that her son should be raised with his paternal family may well have been amicable.

Leofric is also recorded in the *Liber Eliensis* as having had a brother called Ethelnoth. This Ethelnoth is even more shadowy than his brother, although there is evidence that there may have been some bad feeling between the two. When Leofric founded a new church at Eynesbury, his uncle, Ealdorman Ethelwine, gave land at Wangford to the foundation.[37] Ethelnoth later tried to claim that this land was his inheritance and sought its return, only for Ethelwine to angrily produce evidence that he had bought the lands, presumably from Leofric himself. Given this family dispute over their inheritance, it may be that the brothers were the sons of different wives, since Ethelwold may have been married before. Alternatively, Ethelnoth may also have been Elfrida's son. Again, there is no evidence of Elfrida having any contact with him.

Ethelwold is also known to have had a daughter named Ethelflaed or Elfflaed.[38] It is uncertain whether Ethelflaed was Elfrida's daughter or not. One tradition records that Ethelwold had previously been married to a noblewoman named Brithwina by whom he had several children.[39] In another account, the lady in question was called Brihtgifu.[40] Ethelflaed was apparently Ethelwold's youngest daughter, with one account suggesting that she was a posthumous child, something that would indicate that she was Elfrida's.[41] Another indication that she might have been Elfrida's daughter is the fact that in a fourteenth-century manuscript containing a Life of Ethelflaed, her mother was described as 'a young lady discreet in manners and handsome in form, and near of kin to his [Edgar's] wife, Queen Elfrida'.[42] The writer was entirely unaware of Elfrida's first marriage to Ethelwold and vague about her exact relationship to Ethelflaed, something that might suggest that Elfrida was in fact her mother – by the fourteenth century Elfrida's reputation was so poor that it might not have been deemed appropriate for Ethelflaed, who was one of the patron saints of Romsey, to be recorded as her daughter.

Whether her daughter or stepdaughter, Elfrida retained custody of the girl following Ethelwold's death and it was she and her second husband, King Edgar, who provided for the girl's upbringing, arranging for her to be raised in the nunnery at Romsey, which was founded by the king in 966 or 967.[43] Ethelflaed was placed directly under the care of the house's new abbess, St Merewenna. It is unclear how old Ethelflaed was at this time, but the suggestion is that she was young. Certainly, she was not considered suitable to succeed her governess as abbess at her death in 993, instead later becoming the house's third abbess in 996.[44] She was consecrated as a nun by her stepmother's favourite, Bishop Ethelwold, at some point before Edgar's death in 975, when she would have been in her early teens.

In the late tenth century, it was common for aristocratic girls to be raised in nunneries without also being promised to the nunnery, and it is therefore likely that Elfrida did not, at first, envisage a religious life for her stepdaughter. Ethelflaed later came to be considered to be a saint, and a Latin saint's Life exists for her in a manuscript dating to the fourteenth century. From this, it is clear that Ethelflaed was taught in a schoolroom with a number of other young girls, under the care of a female teacher who was not above beating them if they failed to comply with their lessons.[45] In one account of Elfrida's stepdaughter, for example, when she had miraculously been made aware that her teacher intended to beat her and the other girls, Ethelflaed threw herself at her teacher's feet, begging in tears, 'Do not, Mistress, do not beat us with the switches: we will sing and chant at your pleasure, willingly, as much or as long as you wish or command. When we gladly carry out orders, why do you beat us?'[46] Ethelflaed excelled at the religious education she received, although she would also have been taught to read and write and, potentially, to understand other languages such as Latin. As befitted her rank, she was placed under the direct care of the abbess, Merewenna, who quickly became fond of her, desiring 'to have her continually in attendance'.[47] The relationship between the two became close, with Merewenna behaving 'as a most sweet mother to Ethelfleda, and Ethelfleda as a most loving daughter to Merwynna'.[48]

Elfrida, although apparently a somewhat distant figure to her stepdaughter, did remain in contact with her, agreeing to her consecration as a nun. She also brought the girl to visit her at court on occasion before the consecration, suggesting the possibility that she had intended to find her a husband before her vocation became clear. According to Ethelflaed's Life, Elfrida called the girl to stay with her in court in her own chamber. Ethelflaed, who had by then spent some years at Romsey, was unwilling to comply, since she was 'fearful lest the deceitful pleasure of earthly vanities, – which she often saw practised around the queen, as the mannerisms in dress, behaviours, and other things, which are called by the gay, refinement, but which hinder from holy religion, – should recall her mind from her holy purpose'.[49] This was evidently not Ethelflaed's first visit to court and it may be that Elfrida hoped to bring her away from the wholly monastic influence. Elfrida certainly took her duties as a guardian seriously and one night, when she 'could not sleep for thinking', she caught Ethelflaed sneaking out of her chamber and followed her, perhaps not unsurprisingly imagining 'her to be going out for immodest purposes at such an hour of the night'. According to the Life, Ethelflaed was in fact going to immerse herself privately in a spring so that she could pray and sing psalms, and the queen, for her lack of faith in her young stepdaughter, was struck down by God and appeared to lose her senses. It was only Ethelflaed's prayers that brought Elfrida back to her health, something that might have persuaded her to finally give her consent to the girl's consecration.

Whether Ethelflaed was Elfrida's own daughter or not, the evidence suggests that she felt responsible for her and, in all probability, affection. In 968 Edgar gave Romsey the royal estate of Edington in Wiltshire, a gift that benefited his wife's stepdaughter. In addition to this, it was at Romsey that Elfrida's eldest son by the king, the Aetheling

Edmund, was buried in 971, suggesting a close relationship with the house and, in all probability, visits there by the king and queen while Elfrida spent time with Ethelflaed. It has been noted that Elfrida, whose reputation appears to have been particularly smeared by the English nunneries during her lifetime, was favourably portrayed only in works from Romsey, again suggesting an affectionate relationship with Ethelflaed, who later became the house's abbess.[50] She lived to old age and later, after being popularly recognised as a saint, became the joint patron of the nunnery alongside St Mary.

Whether as her mother or her stepmother, Elfrida certainly remained involved in Ethelflaed's life, something that shows her in a very positive light as a mother and belies any claims that she was estranged from her first husband's family during King Edgar's lifetime. More likely, it was agreed following Ethelwold's death that Elfrida would retain custody of his daughters (whether her own or a previous wife's) until their marriages, while any sons were raised by their paternal kin.

One account associated with Romsey Abbey, where Ethelwold's daughter, Ethelflaed, served as abbess, claims that Ethelwold died of a sickness in the presence of his wife, whom he pressed to found a nunnery in Romsey, where they were living.[51] Given the fact that Ethelwold was a monastic benefactor in his own right, as well as being the son of the reform-minded Half-King, this is entirely within character and is further evidence to support the view that he died of natural causes. Elfrida, who may have first become interested in religious reform during her time as Ethelwold's wife, complied, making a gift of a house at Sydmanton in Hampshire, which she had owned with her first husband, to the nunnery. The late tenth-century Life of St Oswald, written by a monk of Ramsey Abbey who was associated with Ethelwold's brother, Ethelwine, also made no mention of Ethelwold being murdered in his work, in spite of discussing Elfrida's first husband and his brothers in great detail. His only comment on Ethelwold's death was the statement regarding Elfrida, that 'a regal bearing was befitting to her, since after the death of [her husband] the distinguished ealdorman [Ethelwold, eldest son of Aethelstan 'Half-King'], she had been found worthy to marry the king', an account containing no hint that she and Edgar had been involved in murder.[52]

Something that probably further demonstrates Elfrida and Edgar's innocence in Ethelwold's murder is the fact that, after his death in 962, Edgar immediately appointed Elfrida's youngest brother-in-law, Ethelwine, to his dead brother's ealdordom.[53] Given the importance to the king of retaining the loyalty of his ealdormen, it is inconceivable that he would have appointed a man with such a grudge against him to this non-hereditary office if he had indeed murdered that man's brother. Edgar and Elfrida were later accused of having committed adultery before their marriage, and it is therefore not impossible that they had begun an affair during Ethelwold's lifetime. However, given Edgar's continuing friendly relations with his other foster brothers, this seems unlikely. There is also no evidence of any hostility between Elfrida and her first husband's family until the reign of her stepson, Edward the Martyr, an estrangement that can be explained by their support for him over her own son, rather than any murder. More likely, accusations of adultery related to the marital status of Edgar rather than Elfrida.

3

KING EDGAR

Elfrida took a second husband two years after Ethelwold's death in 964. While her first marriage had been to a man in the highest rank of the nobility, in her second match she exceeded this, taking the king himself as her husband.

By the mid-tenth century, the kings of Wessex had succeeded in taking, and maintaining, control over most of what would now be considered to be England. The founder of the dynasty, King Ecgbert, had begun the process of unifying England, a process that was completed by his great-grandsons, Kings Athelstan, Edmund and Eadred. These early kings were highly successful, even during the incursions of the Vikings, which plagued the reigns of Ecgbert's grandsons Ethelbald, Ethelberht, Ethelred I and Alfred the Great. By the time Edgar succeeded to the throne in 959, he ruled an area roughly comparable with the bounds of modern England. King Edgar, who has been nicknamed 'the Peaceable', is remembered as one of the most successful, if also the most shadowy, of the Anglo-Saxon kings of England. It was a combination of luck and political manipulation that won him the throne of England.

Edgar was the younger of the two sons born to King Edmund I by his first wife Elfgifu. He was born in around 943 or 944 and, as a result, would have barely known his mother who died in 944, perhaps as a result of complications following her younger son's birth. According to William of Malmesbury, the birth of Elfgifu's last child was particularly auspicious, with the prominent churchman, Dunstan, claiming to hear an angelic voice proclaiming peace at the very moment that Edgar was born.[1] This story seems scarcely credible, although the baby, who, apart from his elder brother, was the only male of his generation in the family, would have been particularly welcomed. A further claim by William of Malmesbury that Edgar was particularly close to his pious mother and turned to her when he had troubling dreams is nonsense: he cannot have remembered her. Elfgifu may well have had a positive posthumous influence on her younger child however. Following her burial at Shaftesbury Abbey, miracles were reported at her tomb and she was popularly regarded as a saint: a somewhat easier route to canonisation than was possible in later periods.[2]

Edgar's father, Edmund, did not remain a widower for long, having taken a noblewoman named Ethelflaed of Damerhan as his second wife by the time of his own death in 946. Ethelflaed was the elder of the two daughters of Ealdorman Elfgar and it appears that her status as an heiress may have been what attracted the king to her. The *Liber Eliensis* referred to her in her old age as 'a very wealthy woman by virtue of her estates, her marriage-portion and the inherited patrimony of her family. Hence she seemed the noblest among her kinsfolk.'[3] Edmund was sufficiently eager to acquire Ethelflaed that he gave her father the gift of a valuable sword worth 120 mancuses of gold, with four pounds of silver on the sheath.[4] In his Will, made during the reign of King Eadred, he left large bequests of land to his two daughters, with Ethelflaed's bequests 'on condition that she be the more zealous for the welfare of my soul and of her mother's soul and of her brother's soul and of her own'. Ethelflaed's younger sister married the powerful Ealdorman Brihtnoth of Essex,[5] while Ethelflaed herself, after she was widowed, took another ealdorman, Athelstan *Rota*, as her second husband.[6]

Ethelflaed was not entrusted with the care of either of her two stepsons. It is possible that the two boys were sent to foster families soon after their mother's death and before their father's remarriage. Ethelflaed's Will suggests a good relationship with the royal family and it would seem that she was on friendly terms with her royal stepchildren. Certainly, although she would outlive Edgar, she left her principal estate of Damerham to Glastonbury, where both Edmund and Edgar were buried, 'for King Edmund's soul and for King Edgar's and for mine. And I grant the estate at Ham to Christchurch, at Canterbury for King Edmund's soul and for my soul.'[7] No reference was made to her deceased second husband in her own Will, perhaps suggesting that she looked back more fondly on her first, royal, union, and the family she acquired through marriage.

Edgar and his elder brother, Eadwig, may have had as limited a memory of their father as they did of their mother. By the twelfth century, King Edmund was revered as 'a good man' and one who was remembered for his martial successes.[8] He is chiefly remembered for fighting bravely alongside his half-brother, King Athelstan, at the Battle of Brunanburh in 937.[9] While Edgar would not have known his father, it is clear that Edmund was a sire of whom to be proud. An epic poem that records details of the battle proclaimed,

King Athelstan, the lord of warriors,
Patron of heroes, and his brother too,
Prince Edmund, won themselves eternal glory
In battle with the edges of their swords
Round Brunanburh; they broke the wall of shields,
The sons of Edward with their well-forged swords
Slashed at the linden-shields; such was their nature
From boyhood that in battle they had often
Fought for their land, its treasures and its homes,
Against all enemies.[10]

Athelstan died in 939 and was succeeded by Edmund, who was some years younger than his elder half-brother. Edmund, like the majority of tenth-century English kings, died young. On the night of 26 May 946, when his youngest son was still an infant, he disturbed a thief at his royal manor of Pucklechurch; the thief, in order to avoid capture, stabbed the king to death.[11] Edmund's death was bloody and sudden, but there are certainly echoes of the later death of his grandson, Edward the Martyr. It would seem that there may have been more to Edmund's death than simply being in the wrong place at the wrong time. Whether Edmund's death was unplanned is not certain, given that Gaimar was later to claim that his brother and successor, Eadred, 'well revenged his brother Eadmund. He avenged him on his enemies who had slain him by murder.'[12] Edmund's elder son, Eadwig, was then a small boy living with his foster father, a thegn named Elric. His younger son, Edgar, was an infant, also fostered out. It would therefore have surprised no one that the succession in 946 followed a precedent set in 871 when the young sons of King Ethelred I were passed over for his brother, Alfred the Great. In 946 Edmund's brother, Eadred, the last surviving son of Edward the Elder, took the throne.

As an infant, Edgar was sent to live with the noblewoman Elfwyn, who was the wife of Athelstan Half-King and Elfrida's future mother-in-law.[13] The Half-King was at the height of his power under Edmund and his brother, Eadred, and this, coupled with Elfwyn's noble background, made the couple entirely suitable as guardians for the young prince. It is also not impossible that the couple's base in East Anglia, as well as their Mercian interests, were considered particularly important in the choice. Wessex and Mercia had only fully become united under one ruler early in the tenth century and there is some evidence that this union might not always have been viewed as permanent. The future King Athelstan, who was the only son of King Edward the Elder's first marriage, was fostered in Mercia by his aunt, the famous Ethelflaed, Lady of the Mercians, and her husband. It appears that Edward viewed his first marriage as less legitimate than his later two matches and it was Elfweard, the eldest son of his second wife, whom he chose as his successor, only for the prince to die very shortly after his father. Athelstan, with his Mercian upbringing, was considered to be his father's successor in Mercia, while his half-brother succeeded to Wessex; a similar scheme may well have been intended for Eadwig and Edgar, particularly as events did, in fact, pan out that way.

Edgar enjoyed a contented upbringing with the Half-King and his wife. Of their four sons, the youngest, Ethelwine, was only three or four years older than him and the pair became close, with Elfrida's youngest brother-in-law being particularly favoured during her second husband's reign.[14] The two boys were probably educated together and their well-known interest in religious reform must have been developed by Athelstan Half-King himself who was deeply involved in monasticism. It was almost certainly the Half-King who arranged for Edgar to go to the newly restored monastery at Abingdon when he was old enough, in order to be tutored by the abbot there, Ethelwold.[15] Ethelwold was one of the leading churchmen involved in the religious reform and a great friend to Elfrida; he instilled in Edgar a love for the Benedictine reform movement. A brief account of his education, probably composed by Abbot Ethelwold himself, confirms this, as does Edgar's own later conduct:

> For while he [Edgar] engaged in the various pursuits that befit boyhood, he was nevertheless touched by the divine regard, being diligently admonished by a certain abbot who explained to him the royal way of the Catholic faith.[16]

Edgar was raised to have a deep regard for the monastic reform then prevalent on the Continent. He remained in East Anglia throughout the brief reign of his uncle, the sickly King Eadred, who died in 955. This death did not change life unduly for Edgar and he stayed at Abingdon for the first year of the reign of his brother, King Eadwig. Given that Abingdon was firmly within the Half-King's sphere of influence, it is not impossible that he first became acquainted with the new bride of his foster brother, Ethelwold. There may well be some truth to the rumours that Edgar became attracted to Elfrida during her first marriage. Alternatively, as set out above, the marriage may have occurred a few years later.

By 956 Edgar was around twelve or thirteen and, in an age where many died young, was considered old enough to take a public role.

During the early years of Eadwig's reign, Edgar appears to have been often at his brother's court enjoying a position of high status. He was a regular witness to charters, often witnessing second after the king and specifically named as the king's brother.[17] Like his brother, he must have cut a prepossessing figure at court, in spite of his youth. One contemporary claimed that Eadwig was nicknamed 'All-Fair' for 'his great beauty', and a handsome appearance, ran in the family.[18] Edgar, although apparently short, was also very strong, a trait that was highly valued in tenth-century England.[19] He first began to appear in the company of his grandmother, Queen Eadgifu, and it has been suggested that she was responsible for overseeing both Eadwig and Edgar's upbringings, a role that Elfrida would later fulfil for her own grandchildren.[20]

According to a tenth-century chronicle written by the nobleman Ethelweard, who just happened to be Eadwig's brother-in-law, the king 'held the kingdom continuously for four years and deserved to be loved'.[21] This is the lone positive assessment of the reign, with all other sources, which were compiled by monastic writers opposed to him, being deeply hostile. The truth lies somewhere in the middle and Eadwig, who can only have been around fifteen or sixteen at his accession, inherited a court divided by political factions due to the long illness of his predecessor, the unmarried King Eadred. Eadred's mother, Queen Eadgifu, had been a particularly dominant force during his reign, aided by her allies Athestan Half-King, Dunstan, the Abbot of Glastonbury and Archbishop Oda of Canterbury. This party was also the party of monastic reform, and while his opposition to the faction's members does not necessarily preclude Eadwig from being as pious as his younger brother, the conflicts that arose immediately with this faction allowed them to paint him in an unholy fashion.

Conflict arose as soon as Eadred was dead, and it seems possible that there may have been a disputed succession, with Eadgifu's monastic party favouring Edgar, who had, of course, been raised by one of their members. Eadwig, who had been raised in Wessex, naturally turned towards West Saxon families and quickly secured an alliance with a powerful Wessex family who were descended from King Ethelred I, the elder brother of Alfred the Great. That this alliance had been finalised by the time of Eadwig's coronation is clear from a scandalous story recorded in an early Life of St Dunstan, written by the cleric Elfric. According to the Life, Eadwig, who showed little aptitude for government, disappeared from the banquet that followed his coronation, instead seeking the 'caresses of loose women'.[22] When his absence was noticed, Dunstan and his kinsman, Bishop Cynesige of Lichfield, volunteered to go and fetch him, finding him in his bedchamber where he was lying with a woman called Ethelgifu and her daughter, Elfgiu, 'wallowing between the two of them in evil fashion'. To add insult to injury, Eadwig had also thrown the royal crown carelessly aside on the floor. Dunstan rebuked the women and forcibly replaced the crown on Eadwig's head, before dragging him back to the banquet. This event is almost certainly an attempt to smear Eadwig and the two women, since Elfgifu, the younger of the two women, was, in fact a woman from a respectable noble house and already his wife. More likely, Dunstan and his friends were angered by the prominence given to Elfgifu and her family at the coronation, who had become the king's own faction and were directly opposed to the monastic party.

In the early years of his reign, Eadwig enjoyed some success in asserting both his own dominance, and that of his wife's party. The retirement to Glastonbury Abbey of Athelstan Half-King, who had ruled almost as a regent under Eadred, was connected with this, although it appears that the Half-King had remained strong enough to negotiate his retirement with the king, ensuring that his eldest son replaced him. Dunstan himself proved to have no such bargaining power, and was exiled in 957 on the young king's orders.[23] The king's grandmother, Eadgifu, 'was despoiled of all her property' and forcibly retired, very much against her will.[24] Her son, King Eadred, had evidently intended that she was to retain her political influence, adding to her already great wealth at his death with the clause in his Will that 'I give to my mother the estates at Amesbury and Wantage and Basing, and all the booklands which I have in Sussex, Surrey and Kent, and all those which she had previously held'.[25]

To depose Eadgifu of her influence and estates was actually quite a formidable task. She had been a teenage heiress when King Edward the Elder had abandoned his royal second wife to marry her, presumably in order to acquire her lands. While she had only limited influence over Edward, being forced to ask her friends to induce him to recover one of her estates, which had been misappropriated,[26] for example, she used her wealth and position effectively in widowhood. One suggestion is that she came to an agreement with her stepson, King Athelstan, to support his bid for the throne in preference to the sons of Edward's still-living second wife, an arrangement that secured the king's recognition of her own young sons as his heirs and his assurance that he would not marry and beget his own children.[27]

In tenth-century England it appears that there could only be one queen at any time, and the fact that an attempt was made to replace Eadgifu with Elfgifu would account for much of the very personal hostility directed at the king's young bride. Eadwig entirely refused to aid his grandmother in any of her disputes, as can be seen from her own complaint in a legal case that, after Eadred's death, two estates that she had inherited from her father and over which ownership had long been disputed by a man named Goda, were seized by Goda's sons. According to Eadgifu's own account, these men 'told the young prince Eadwig, who had been proclaimed king, that they had a juster claim to them than she'.[28] It was only with Edgar's accession and Eadgifu's return to favour that she was able to have it declared that the sons had committed 'wicked robbery', and take the lands back into her own possession. Eadwig's decision to inter his uncle at Winchester, contrary to the funeral wishes expressed in his Will, was probably a more personal move against his grandmother. That the young king was opposed to the individuals rather than what they represented can be seen in the continued favour shown to Ethelwold, Abbot of Abingdon.[29]

If Eadwig's succession had indeed been disputed, then the fact of his marriage and the possibility that Elfgifu might bear him a son must have been of great concern to Eadgifu's party. In spite of the exile or retirement of its leading members, the group remained powerful, recruiting Edgar himself to their cause. The exact events of 957 are not clear. According to the twelfth-century chronicle once attributed to Florence of Worcester, in that year, Eadwig's ineptitude as a ruler led to the Mercians and Northumbrians deserting him in disgust, and choosing Edgar as their king, splitting the country in two.[30] Whether this was the result of a coup or Edgar's supporters enforcing a long-planned scheme of joint kingship[31] is not certain, but either way it can hardly have been welcomed by Eadwig, who had previously been crowned king of all England. Edgar issued charters as King of Mercia and certainly accepted the role with enthusiasm, recruiting a number of leading noblemen, such as Elfrida's own husband, Ealdorman Ethelwold, to his cause.

The establishment of Edgar's kingdom also completely destabilised Eadwig's kingdom south of the Thames, with the success of the monastic party made clear in 958 when Archbishop Oda divorced the king from his wife on the grounds of consanguinity, sending the unfortunate Elfgifu into exile. Given that the couple only shared descent through their great-great-grandparents, King Ethelwulf and his wife, Osburh, and that closer royal marriages were known, it is clear that this was merely an excuse to alienate the king from his own supporters. Eadwig had already taken fruitless steps to appease his brother's party, for example in 957 making a grant of land at Ely to Archbishop Oda.[32] He struggled on for a year after his divorce, apparently making a vain attempt to return to power following Oda's death in 958 with the immediate appointment of his own candidate. He was never in a position to challenge Edgar or recall Elfgifu, however, and he died, rather conveniently, in 959, probably aged only around twenty.

Eadwig's death left Edgar as the sole male-line descendant of Alfred the Great, and it was therefore no surprise that the sixteen-year-old immediately assumed control of the whole of England. There is no evidence that Edgar was crowned before 973, but it seems highly likely that he received a first coronation soon after his accession, as his brother had done. Although, in some respects, Edgar had been raised to be a serious-minded and religious young man, this was only one side of his character. To his ecclesiastical supporters' chagrin, he also had another abiding interest: his love of women.

Edgar's marital history was complicated, and it is difficult to number his wives and the mothers of his children. In the twelfth century, Gaimar recorded of Edgar:

The king was wise and valiant.
By his queen he had many fair children.
One so he had of whom I can tell.
This was Eadward of Shaftesbury;
And his daughter was named St Edith,
The lady whom God blessed.
Besides he had three other sons.
From three mothers they were born.
Three mothers had these three.
The king was fond of women.
When his wife died,
He ruined his life through women.[33]

Gaimar presents a rather confused picture, apparently believing that both Edward the Martyr and St Edith were the children of one mother, Edgar's queen, who bore a number of children before dying. In addition to this, the chronicler considered that Edgar had three other sons, all born to different women. That this first queen was not believed to be Elfrida is clear from the fact that, in his history, Gaimar then went on to discuss her relationship with the king.

The main difficulty in assessing the facts behind Edgar's unions is due to a changing definition of what constituted a marriage. In the Anglo-Saxon period it was possible for a type of marriage to exist that was not sanctioned by the Church and that the Church came to consider a concubinage. Such a relationship could be considered as much a marriage as one blessed in church, but it was also possible for the exact nature of the relationship to be denigrated and for the wife and children to be considered to be illegitimate. Equally, the status of the bride may well have had an effect on the legitimacy of the union: King Athelstan was the product of a non-Church-sanctioned marriage and rumours were circulated by those opposed to his accession that his mother was the daughter of a shepherd and a mere concubine.

Edgar is usually supposed to have taken his first wife at around the time of his accession to the throne in Mercia, a move that would have been taken to help build support. This wife appears in no contemporary records, although a later medieval chronicler claimed that she was called Ethelflaed *Eneda* (which means swan or fair) or *Candida* (white) and that she was the daughter of an ealdorman named Ordmaer.[34] The assumption with these nicknames must be that Ethelflaed was beautiful, something that would certainly have recommended her to Edgar. It has been pointed out that the only document appearing to corroborate this claim is a twelfth-century list of benefactors of the New Minster at Winchester, which names her as Edgar's wife, but this is doubtful.[35] She is traditionally said to have been the mother of Edgar's son, Edward, who was still not considered to be a man in 975 at the time of his father's death, something that would suggest a date of birth at the earliest around 960 or 961. It would certainly seem that Edward was born after Eadwig's death, given the fact that Edgar was considered to be a man by at least the age of sixteen.

Based on the age of Edward, if Ethelflaed can, indeed, be identified as his mother, then she remained Edgar's wife for at least a year or so after his accession to the throne of all England, making the suggestion that she had been married merely to provide Edgar with support as King of Mercia unlikely. There is, in fact, no evidence that she came from a powerful Mercian family. That said, however, if Ethelflaed was the daughter of Thegn Ordmaer of Hatfield, as discussed earlier, then she is highly likely to have been a cousin of Elfrida. It made strong political sense for Ealdorman

Ethelwold, with his Mercian interests, to marry Elfrida, so perhaps there is some truth in the suggestion that Edgar selected her kinswoman as his first wife to shore up his position in Mercia.

Given Ethelflaed's almost complete absence from the sources, the question must be asked as to whether she existed at all. Royal women of the house of Wessex were often particularly shadowy, something that had led to folklore building up around the royal house about a murderous ninth-century queen who had brought the office of queen into disrepute. There is reason for doubting her existence. No ealdorman called Ordmaer is known to have existed, and the similarity in the name of Ordmaer to that of Elfrida's father, Ordgar, is suspicious, particularly since Gaimar claimed that Elfrida was nicknamed 'Elfrida the Fair', a name very close to 'Ethelflaed the Fair/Swan or White', suggesting that a tradition of a first wife may have developed out of the facts of Elfrida's own life.

This is hardly conclusive, however; a thegn called Ordmaer did exist, with a close enough relationship to Edgar to bequeath land to him – perhaps in fulfilment of Ethelflaed's dowry? This Ordmaer was also described in the *Liber Eliensis* as a 'powerful man', and he and his wife Ealde may well have been of sufficient wealth and status to be the parents-in-law of the king. Similarly, nicknaming a royally connected woman to imply beauty was hardly uncommon – the later Harold II's first wife/concubine was known as Edith Swan-Neck, for example. It is true that the later *Passion of St Edward* portrayed its subject as the son of Wulfthryth, a wife of Edgar's who was the mother of his daughter, St Edith. However, claims that Edith regarded Edward as her full brother do not seem to have any real basis – the eleventh-century Life of St Edith refers to both Edward and Ethelred as her brothers when, clearly, Ethelred is known to have a different mother. This source also makes no reference to Wulfthryth having borne another child, declaring instead that Edith was 'the only child of her mother'.[36]

There is one contemporary document that might suggest what happened to Ethelflaed *Eneda*. A late tenth-century Will survives for a woman named Wynflaed, who was associated with the nunneries at both Wilton and Shaftesbury, but appears to have had particular links to Shaftesbury, possibly having taken vows there.[37] It is not certain who Wynflaed is, although there is one very clear candidate. King Edgar's maternal grandmother is known to have been a woman named Wynflaed, who was close enough to her daughter, Queen Elfgifu, to make gifts in her memory. She is also known to have taken religious vows in her old age. Edgar's mother, St Elfgifu, was buried at Shaftesbury and this would therefore seem a logical place for her mother to support and, perhaps, retire to in her old age. There must be a very strong suspicion, therefore, that Wynflaed the testatrix should be indentified as Wynflaed the royal grandmother.[38] Certainly, much in the Will would support this. Wynflaed was evidently very wealthy, for example making a gift of an engraved bracelet and brooch to a daughter, as well as cups with lids, gold-adorned wooden cups, and even fine curtains and bed clothes to other beneficiaries. She held a number of slaves, including her own weaver and seamstress, and would presumably have often appeared very finely dressed. She was able to give one pound of gold to the nuns at Wilton. Interestingly, among her many bequests, she added 'and to Aethelflaed the White her ... gown and cap and headband, and afterwards Aethelflaed is to supply from her nun's vestments the best she can for Wulfflaed and Aethelgifu and supplement it with gold so that each of them shall have at least sixty pennyworth'. Ethelflaed was a common name and, in fact, Wynflaed had a daughter called Ethelflaed, who was a beneficiary of the Will. The Will also refers to a further Ethelflaed, daughter of Ealhelm. However, it does appear from the wording of the Will that this Ethelflaed the White was a third person, with her nickname given to distinguish her from the others. If so, this Ethelflaed the White would be roughly contemporary with Ethelflaed *Eneda*. She was the beneficiary of a Will highly likely to be that of Edgar's grandmother, and a nun, most likely at Shaftesbury, a convent in which Wynflaed was heavily involved. Was this Ethelflaed *Eneda*?

Shaftesbury would not be an unlikely place for a discarded wife of Edgar to retire to. The settlement, which is 20 miles from the major town of Salisbury, was founded by Alfred the Great when he built a nunnery there for his daughter, Elfgifu, who was a nun.[39] The nunnery retained its royal connections and it has been suggested that the niece of this Elfgifu, Elfwyn of Mercia, was also deposited there by her uncle, King Edward the Elder, when he took direct control of her inheritance of Mercia.[40] Edgar's own mother, St Elfgifu, was buried at the abbey and may, perhaps, have retired there before her death. She certainly came to be associated as a patron saint of the abbey and her mother, Wynflaed, made a gift of land to the nunnery, perhaps in memory of the daughter she survived. It was later specifically chosen to be the final resting place of Edward the Martyr. Wulfthryth, an abandoned wife of Edgar's, retired to Wilton nunnery with her daughter, Edith, following her divorce, and became abbess, which suggests that if she was indeed the mother of Edward it would be more logical for him to be buried in her convent. It therefore does seem entirely plausible to suggest that Edward was indeed the child of a brief first marriage to Ethelflaed and that she retired to the royal nunnery at Shaftesbury following her divorce in order to live the life of a nun.

It was certainly no easy feat to transport the corpse of Edward the Martyr from his grave at Wareham to Shaftesbury in February 979: given the poor winter weather and difficult terrain, it has been estimated that the journey took at least a week, something which is suggested by the fact that, at Shaftesbury, 13 February was observed as the day of translation of St Edward, 18 February as his advent and 20 February as his octave.[41] The choice of Shaftesbury for Edward's burial is otherwise not clear. One recent writer on the history of the abbey commented that 'one can but wonder why the young king was buried in a nunnery and why his remains were brought from Wareham to Shaftesbury'.[42] Perhaps the answer lies in the fact that his mother still remained there as a nun or, at least, that she had lived out her last years there.

It would not be unusual for the king's grandmother to be close to his former wife, and Wynflaed may also have intended, by her gift, to compensate Ethelflaed for the end of her marriage. There is strong evidence that Wynflaed was heavily involved in the arrangements for Edgar's second marriage: a match that appears to have been close to her own heart. Edgar must have taken his second wife very soon after his eldest son, Edward, was born. It is very clear from the stories surrounding this marriage that he desired to make a political alliance, to be sealed by a marriage, rather than a love match. Certainly, he was not particularly concerned about which member of the chosen family he took as his bride.

In the eleventh century, the churchman, Goscelin of St Bertin, who was a chaplain at Wilton Abbey, wrote a number of saints' Lives, including those of Edgar's daughter, St Edith of Wilton, and her older kinswoman, St Wulfhild of Barking. These two saints' Lives, although written more than a century after the events they describe, were based on traditions current in the late Anglo-Saxon and early Norman period, particularly at Wilton Abbey itself, which was very much central to Edgar's search for a second wife.

Edgar's second wife, Wulfthryth, was a member of a prominent noble family in which all the known members' names began with the letter 'W' and, usually, with the first element 'Wulf', something that suggests that they had a very strong naming tradition (in a similar way to the use of 'Ord' as the first element of names in Elfrida's family).[43] Wilton was traditionally founded by Ealdorman Weohstan of Wiltshire, and remained connected with the ealdormanry of that part of England. Wulfhere, Ealdorman of Wiltshire in the late ninth century, is believed to have been the brother of a Queen Wulfthryth who was the wife of the short-lived Ethelred I. His grandson Wulfgar also became an ealdorman of an area that included Wiltshire. Although it cannot be proven, a connection with Wilton between Wulfthryth and other members of her family, along with her name and her political desirability, does suggest that she was a member of this family. If so, Edgar's predecessor, Ethelred I, had seen fit to marry into the family and, with their powerful contacts in central Wessex, they would have made a useful alliance, particularly as the previously Mercian-based Edgar needed to build up a support base in Wessex following Eadwig's death.

Wulfthryth was not, in fact, Edgar's first choice of a bride, with the king instead choosing her kinswoman, Wulfhild. According to the Life of St Wulfhild, in the early 960s an aunt of both Wulfhild and Wulfthryth, named Wenflaed, was living at Wherwell. Wenflaed is commonly supposed to have been an abbess but, in fact, there is no reference in the Life of her having this rank, or even of her living in a nunnery. Goscelin merely claimed that Wenflaed had a house there in the village. It has therefore been suggested that she may have been a woman who had taken a vow of chastity, but was not actually a nun.[44] Wenflaed was the driving force behind arranging the alliance for Edgar and, while this might be motivated by her desire to ensure that a niece of hers became queen, there may be another reason for her active involvement.

The Life of St Wulfhild claims that Wulfhild and Wulfthryth were sisters and that both were the daughters of a Wulfhelm, who was a brother of Edgar's father. In the Life of St Edith, Goscelin further elaborated, calling Wulfthryth a descendant of princes and the daughter of an ealdorman.[45] King Edmund I was a son of Edward the Elder, and there is no evidence that either Edward or his third wife, Eadgifu, had a son called Wulfhelm, particularly since there is no evidence that such a name was ever used by the royal family. However, it is possible that Goscelin's error was merely about the descent of Wulfhelm rather than the relationship. Edgar's maternal grandmother, as outlined above, was Wynflaed, who took a religious vow in her old age and would fit very well with Goscelin's description of Wulfthryth's Aunt Wenflaed. Given that he believed the couple to be cousins, it seems plausible that they were, i.e. that Wulfthryth and Wulfhild's aunt was also Edgar's grandmother. This would explain the woman's keen interest in the match, and also may have been the grounds upon which the marriage was eventually brought to an end. While cousin marriages could be frowned upon, as that of Eadwig and Elfgifu showed, they did occur: Edgar's grandfather, Edward the Elder, for example, took Elfflaed, the daughter of his first cousin, as his second wife at around the time of his accession to the throne. Assuming that Wenflaed the aunt and Wynflaed the grandmother were the same person, it becomes clear why Edgar was so keen to further ally himself with the family: connected to the descendants of Ethelred I, this family had been deemed a suitable match for his father and he was clearly following the same policy on his own accession.

It would therefore appear that Edgar went to his grandmother Wynflaed to request her help in arranging a match with one of her nieces. She suggested Wulfhild who, like her kinswoman Wulfthryth, was being educated at Wilton Abbey. Wilton has been described as an upper-class boarding school, and for a girl to be sent there was no indication that it was intended that she would become a nun.[46] Edgar's daughter, St Edith, for example, was educated there but does not appear to have become a nun.[47] Her namesake, Edith the wife of Edward the Confessor, was also raised there and certainly took no holy vows. Wulfhild, who considered herself a nun, or at least to have such a vocation, refused to countenance marriage. However, Edgar, not to be deterred, turned once again to his grandmother, who called the girl to her house in Wherwell, pretending that she was dying and needed the girl to write her Will for her. On her arrival, Wulfhild was shocked to be met by Edgar, who embraced her passionately. She fled to her own rooms, only for her aunt to lock her in the chamber until she agreed to marry the king. Wulfhild was not to be deterred and made her way home through the house's sewers. This may have shown both Edgar and his grandmother just how final Wulfhild's answer was. When he finally abandoned his attempts to seduce Wulfhild, Edgar, perhaps to demonstrate his compliance to her powerful family, gave her the nunnery of Barking over which to be abbess.

According to the Life of Wulfhild he also accepted a substitute bride with good grace. Goscelin wrote that the king, having given up Wulfhild, accepted by divine dispensation his kinswoman Wulfthryth, the daughter of his father's brother Wulfhelm. She had been educated in secular clothing in the same monastery as Wulfhild had been, and was of equal reputation for beauty and nobility and equally worthy by her birth and breeding of the king and of royal power.[48]

Although, through her lineage, Wulfthryth was a suitable choice, there was a potential bar to the relationship. As Edgar's pursuit of Wulfhild had shown, there was some ambiguity over the status of girls educated in nunneries, with some dedicated to the nunnery as nuns and others not. The twelfth-century William of Malmesbury, for example, considered that Edgar was often prey to lust and Wulfthryth is almost certainly the young nun of Wilton described in the Life of St Dunstan. According to the Life, Edgar fell in love with a young nun and made her his mistress, in spite of the fact that he was married and she was a nun.[49] Perhaps in a reference to the still-living Ethelflaed *Eneda*, the Life did not consider Wulfthyth to be Edgar's wife, instead claiming that he was only married twice. It seems probable that it was confusion over whether or not Wulfthryth was a nun that led to later sources referring to her only as a concubine of the king's. William of Malmesbury, probably remembering the example of his contemporary queen, Matilda of Scotland, who had also been accused of being a nun before her marriage, claimed decisively that Wulfthryth

was not actually a nun, as popular opinion crazily supposes. She had merely put on the veil as her own idea in her sudden fear of the king, before, as the story continues, the king snatched away the veil and dragged her to his bed. Because he had touched a woman, who had been a nun, if only potentially, he was reproved by St Dunstan and made to do penance for seven years.[50]

The idea of a penance was introduced to account for Edgar's coronation in 973, long after he had succeeded to the throne. It has no basis in fact, but does demonstrate the difficulties that later writers had in seeing the convent-educated Wulfthryth as a wife.

Edgar and Wulfthryth were married by around 961, and the new queen bore a daughter, Edith, at the royal estate at Kemsing in Kent, either in that year or the next. Edgar welcomed his daughter, arranging for her to be baptised by Dunstan, who was by then Archbishop of Canterbury, in the presence of the leading men of the country.[51] According to William of Malmesbury, Wulfthryth was a reluctant wife who 'did not develop a taste for repetitions of sexual pleasure, but rather shunned them in disgust', and retired to Wilton with her daughter soon after the birth.[52] William of Malmesbury was at pains to stress the voluntary nature of Wulfthryth's retirement, something that was echoed in the Life of St Edith, with the claim that Wulfthryth wished to become a nun and enlisted the support of Abbot Ethelwold, who was by then Bishop of Winchester, to assist her. This would place the divorce after 963, when Ethelwold took control of his see, something that is also supported by Goscelin's claim that Edith was two at the time of her parents' divorce.[53] He was later very firmly allied with Elfrida, and it does therefore seem to be possible that Ethelwold, acting in this way in the divorce, intended to clear the way for Elfrida to marry the king the following year. With Ethelwold's support, space was made for Wulfthryth to retire honourably to Wilton as its abbess:

She left an earthly kingdom and bridal and came to the monastery of the virginal mother of God; in place of the gold-embroidered purple she was clothed in the black tunic of one who was a pilgrim of the Lord; in the place of gold jewellery she was adorned with modesty; in place of a regal diadem she was covered with a dark veil.[54]

Wulfthryth was also permitted to retire with some ceremony, being escorted by Edgar and his court.[55] When the party reached Wilton the entire town came out to watch the procession as it wended its way to the church. With great ceremony, both Wulfthryth and her toddler daughter laid aside their secular clothes and possessions; Edith, in particular, gained admiration for choosing a veil from among the splendid clothes laid out. It was the last moment that Edgar and Wulfthryth appeared together as a couple, with the people assembled offering 'congratulations and joy for her [Edith's] father and mother' at her display of piety. Due to the power of her family, Wulfthryth's consent to retire must have been dearly bought, and it is perhaps telling that, at the same time, Edgar made an 'offering' of his daughter to her mother, confirming that she would be permitted to stay with her and remain 'in the bosom of her mother'. Wulfthryth was also remembered at Wilton for being extremely wealthy and it would seem that she received a large divorce settlement. For the couple to have divorced only two or three years after their marriage, and almost immediately before Edgar's marriage to Elfrida, suggests that the divorce was intended to clear the way for the king's third match.

Given the political nature of Wulfthryth and Edgar's marriage, it is perhaps not surprising that the king continued to take mistresses for its duration. William of Malmesbury, for example, had heard of one such woman, recording that the king was visiting Andover in Hampshire one day when he decided to send for the daughter of a local nobleman who was famed for her beauty.[56] The girl's mother was horrified at the thought of her daughter becoming the married king's mistress and, instead, sent a servant girl to impersonate her. Edgar and the servant girl spent the night together and it was only in the morning when the girl attempted to leave to attend to her duties that Edgar realised that he had been duped. Angered, the maid was

> retained, though with difficulty, on her knees, she bewailed her wretched situation to the king, and entreated her freedom as the recompense of her connection with him, saying that it became his greatness not to suffer one who had ministered to his royal pleasure any longer to groan under the commands of cruel masters. His indignation being excited, and sternly smiling, while his mind was wandering between pity to the girl and displeasure to her mistress, he at last, as if treating the whole as a joke, released her from servitude, and dismissed his anger. Soon after he exalted her, with great honour, to be mistress of her former tyrants, whether they liked it or not; he loved her entirely, nor left her bed until he took Elfrida, the daughter of Ordgar, to be his legitimate wife.

Elfrida had a strong enough hold over the king for him to dismiss his longstanding mistress and she was certainly able to persuade him to dismiss his wife. This all supports the view that Edgar and Elfrida made a love match, with Gaimar recording that 'he loved her. She held him dear.'[57]

Although Wulfthryth consented to the ending of her marriage and retired with grace to a comfortable life in a convent, her continued existence must always have been a concern to Edgar and Elfrida. One historian has recently pointed out that, although Anglo-Saxon custom allowed a spouse to remarry if their wife became a nun, a stricter view of canon law arguably meant that any later remarriage was illegitimate.[58] Almost certainly, this is the basis for the claim advanced against Elfrida very shortly after her second marriage – that she and Edgar were committing adultery.

4

ELFRIDA'S MARRIAGE AND QUEENSHIP

For Elfrida, life changed in 964 when she and Edgar, who had become acquainted perhaps as early as the time of her first marriage, took the decision to marry. Even more momentously, unlike his previous marriages, Edgar took the decision to make his third wife his queen.

At some point after the death of her first husband, Edgar sent for Elfrida, apparently intending to marry her.[1] Elfrida had been staying with her father in Devon and travelled to join the court at Gloucester where the king had assembled a large company. According to Gaimar, she made a great show of her lineage and wealth, appearing richly dressed and accompanied by noblemen from Somerset, Devon, Dorset and Cornwall, all of whom were tenants of her father. She also brought many members of her family, who were hoping for advancement. Elfrida herself had dressed to reflect her hopes of becoming queen:

> What shall I say of her attire?
> She had a ring on her finger
> Which was worth more alone

Than all her dress.
She wore a cape of black silk
Which trailed along the hall.
Over this she wore a mantle,
Within, grey fur, without, blue.
Of other stuff was her robe.
She was very fair.[2]

The couple had evidently already reached an agreement to marry, as Elfrida arrived dressed as a future queen. Edgar took her by the hands and led her to her chamber, keeping her close beside him since 'under heaven there was nothing he held so dear'. Very early the following morning the couple were married privately in the king's chapel, attended only by his household priests.

Once the marriage ceremony had been performed, Edgar, who was himself lavishly dressed in his 'royal raiment', called for his thegns to witness the new queen, dressed as richly as he. According to Gaimar, the king wore a crown of gold and Elfrida also appeared crowned, something that might suggest that her marriage ceremony was accompanied by a ceremony of consecration. Certainly, at the feast that followed the wedding, Gaimar recorded that Elfrida was 'crowned and well served', she was given reverence as queen. Even allowing for considerable poetic licence, there may be some element of truth in the story: a court at Gloucester was by no means unlikely and its proximity to Devon does make it a potential location for Elfrida's marriage. In one twentieth-century analysis of Gaimar's account of Edgar and Elfrida, it was considered that the story came from the traditions of Wherwell Abbey.[3] Since Elfrida would later found this nunnery, it is very likely that they would have had further detail of her life, now lost.

The triumph of the wedding did not last long. Less than a month later, in London, while the couple were lying in a bed curtained with crimson cloth, Archbishop Dunstan burst into the room early in the morning and leaned on the bedpost. According to Gaimar, Edgar asked Dunstan what he wanted, only for the churchman to respond by asking who was with him in the bed. Edgar, of course, replied, 'It is the Queen, Aelfthryth, to whom this kingdom is attached.'[4] Dunstan, however, shook his head, declaring, 'That is false. Better it were that you were dead than to lie thus in adultery, your souls will go to torment.' Elfrida was furious as she lay listening to this and, according to Gaimar, 'she became so sore his enemy that she never loved him more in her life'. Given that Dunstan appears to have previously opposed Edgar's marriage to Wulfthryth, it may be that Elfrida was accused of committing adultery with the husband of Ethelflaed *Eneda*, something that would explain the very particular measures taken by Edgar to demonstrate that it was Elfrida who was his legitimate wife, and not the mother of his eldest son. Alternatively, Dunstan's accusation may relate to the origins of the couple's relationship during Elfrida's first marriage, although if so, it would seem unlikely that Edgar would have waited so long to marry her after Ethelwold's death in 962, particularly since by that date Wulfthryth had already given birth to her only child.

Faced with the opposition of the leading English churchman, Edgar and Elfrida faced something of an uphill battle to establish her as queen rather than just the king's wife. The status of royal women in Wessex was traditionally low, with Asser, the contemporary biographer of King Alfred, feeling able to assert with confidence that the West Saxons had no queens. According to Asser, this custom originated at the very beginning of the ninth century:

The elders of the land maintain that this disputed and indeed infamous custom originated on account of a certain grasping and wicked queen of the same people, who did everything she could against her lord and the whole people, so that not only did she earn hatred for herself, leading to her expulsion from the queen's throne, but she also brought the same foul stigma on all the queens who came after her. For as a result of her very great wickedness, all the inhabitants of the land swore that they would never permit any king to reign over them who had during his lifetime invited the queen to sit beside him on the royal throne.[5]

Although based on highly improbable accounts of the life of an earlier Queen Eadburh, whose posthumous reputation rivals Elfrida's own, by the tenth century Asser's explanation for a lack of queens was popularly accepted. Neither of Edgar's two previous wives were acknowledged as queen or witnessed any charters; theirs were positions identical to the wives of Edgar's father. Only Eadwig's wife, Elfgifu, witnessed an extant charter during her husband's lifetime before Elfrida, but she witnessed as the king's wife rather than as a queen. Even the powerful Eadgifu only begins to appear in charters during the reigns of her sons. At best, a king's wife seems to have been content with the title of *hlaefdige*, or lady.[6] Admittedly, the title 'lady' was used so often in sources for a royal woman that it can almost be translated as queen. However, given that a separate word for queen in Old English exists, there must have been a distinction. It would appear that this was consecration, particularly since the highest-status queens during their husband's lifetime, Elfrida and, later, Emma of Normandy and Edith Godwin, all appear to have been crowned. Other earlier queens also gained status through consecration, and it would seem likely that Asser's story was developed more to explain the West Saxon reaction to a contemporary of his, Judith of Francia, than to record the history of the notorious Queen Eadburh.

Judith of Francia was the first West Saxon queen known to have been consecrated. She was the second wife of Alfred the Great's father, King Ethelwulf; the couple married in Francia in 856. The marriage ceremony was followed immediately by the consecration of the twelve-year-old bride by the Bishop of Reims, a highly unusual ceremony and one that was doubtless insisted upon by the bride's powerful father, Charles the Bald, King of the Franks. The ceremony laid considerable emphasis on the bride's fertility, and was probably intended to enhance the throne-worthiness of any child born to this consecrated mother, over that of the children of Ethelwulf's first marriage. This was how it was viewed in England since Ethelbald, the king's eldest son, rebelled on hearing the news of the marriage, leading to Wessex being divided in two. When his father died a few years later, he took the precaution of marrying his stepmother himself in order to secure a consecrated queen as the mother of his own offspring.

Two other queens of Wessex may also have been crowned. The wife of Ethelred I was referred to as 'Wulfthryth *Regina*' in one charter, suggesting consecration.[7] Although little is known of her, her son felt entitled enough to lay claim to the throne after the death of Alfred the Great, perhaps suggesting that he viewed himself as having an enhanced status through his mother. Similarly, Edward the Elder's chosen successor was his second son, Elfweard, who was the eldest child of his wife, Elfflaed, the granddaughter of Queen Wulfthryth. There is evidence to suggest that Elfflaed shared her husband's coronation, something her powerful family would have been likely to have insisted on.[8]

Gaimar's suggestion that Elfrida was consecrated immediately after her marriage is highly likely to be correct, particularly given the insistence later shown that she and her children were Edgar's legitimate family. If so, a coronation in 964 would have been the first time that a woman was crowned as Queen of England. It is likely to have emphasised Elfrida's expected fertility and may have been similar in form to the consecration of her daughter-in-law, Queen Emma, who underwent the ceremony during her first pregnancy. Another queen who may, perhaps, have been crowned is Edgar's stepmother, Ethelflaed of Damerham, who was described in the Anglo-Saxon Chronicle at Edmund's death as 'his queen'. Her influence is likely to be behind the sudden rise up the charter witness lists of her second husband, Ealdorman Athelstan *Rota*, between 968 and 970. This may, in all likelihood, be the duration of their marriage and suggests reflected prestige for the husband of a dowager queen.

Elfrida would also have had a very recent example of a powerful queen, albeit one who attained power through her sons rather than her husband. Edgar's grandmother, who was still very much alive in 964, had been the first powerful queen mother of the house of Wessex and, although never consecrated, was vastly influential. She witnessed a number of her sons' charters, as well as receiving land grants from them. Eadgifu was also a beneficiary of the Will of Bishop Theodred in the 940s or 950s, receiving the gift of 50 marks of red gold.[9] Such a gift to a royal donee was often made with an agenda in mind and, through looking at surviving Wills, Elfrida's marriage allowed her to replace her grandmother-in-law. For example, the ex-queen, Elfgifu, made Elfrida the bequest of a necklace, an armlet, a drinking cup and 120 mancuses of gold. Another comtemporary Will by the noble couple Brihtric and Elfswith declared that they gave 'to the queen an armlet of thirty mancuses of gold, and a stallion, for her advocacy that the will might stand'.[10] They may have had good reason to enlist her support, having previously called upon Eadgifu and other powerful members of the court to witness a bequest of a manor at Snodland to the Church. After the testator's death this land was subject to a lawsuit between the Church and members of their family, something in which they hoped to obtain Elfrida's protection.[11]

It appears that Elfrida had a good deal of power over whether or not a person's Will was adhered to, a power that the king also enjoyed; in the Will of her kinsman, Ealdorman Elfheah, Elfrida is expressly listed as one of the witnesses to the king granting the testator the necessary permission to even make a Will.[12] A later testator, Leofgifu, who was a member of Queen Emma's household, prudently addressed her Will to her mistress, again demonstrating the power a queen could wield, in relation to just how effective the documents proved to be.[13] Eadgifu dominated the office of queen and it was therefore fortunate for Elfrida that Eadgifu was living in semi-retirement by the time of her own marriage. The two women seem to have been friendly, with the elder queen making Elfrida a gift of land at Holland in Essex when she died, which the younger woman then donated to the monastery at Ely.[14] Eadgifu apparently considered Elfrida to be an appropriate successor to the role that she had created for herself.

Two eleventh-century descriptions survive of just what made the perfect Anglo-Saxon queen, giving some idea of what the role may have been considered to have entailed during Elfrida's time. The first, given in the *Encomium Emmae Reginae*, which was commissioned by Elfrida's daughter-in-law, Emma, considered that a queen was 'a lady of the greatest nobility and wealth, but yet the most distinguished of the women of her time for delightful beauty and wisdom'.[15] The second, provided in the Life of King Edward who Rests at Westminster and commissioned by Queen Edith Godwin, considered that a queen was 'a woman to be placed before all noble matrons or persons of royal and imperial rank as a model of virtue and integrity for maintaining both the practices of the Christian religion and worldy dignity'.[16] Edith saw herself as an advisor to her husband, recalling that 'she was in all the royal counsels, as we might say, a governess and the fount of all goodness, strongly preferring the king's interests to power and riches'.[17] It seems likely that this position was exaggerated. Certainly, for all her status, Elfrida did not reach the height of her power until after Edgar's death. Nonetheless, even with limits, she was politically prominent enough to be permitted to witness a number of charters during the reign, something that demonstrates that she was also present at the important meetings of the royal court. The record of her political involvement is also somewhat skewed by the fact that half of the surviving charters of Edgar's reign date to the period before Elfrida's marriage:[18] what can be said with certainly is that Elfrida's two predecessors as Edgar's wife witnessed none of them.

The court in Anglo-Saxon times was very mobile,[19] and Elfrida would have moved with it, with her clothes and other possessions carefully packed in chests, such as those mentioned in the Will of her contemporary, Wynflaed.[20] For most of the time, the king and his immediate entourage stayed at various royal manors, attended by his household. Several times a year the king would call for a more major assembly, requiring members of the clergy and nobility to travel to meet with him to discuss some item of business, and it was at these that charters were often produced. For Elfrida, these occasions, which often coincided with church festivals, were a chance to demonstrate her queenship to those that mattered.

A major part of the role of a queen was to ensure that both she and the king looked sufficiently regal and, after her marriage, Elfrida joined Edgar on the royal throne when they were at court.[21] It was also important to dress according to her new status, with Elfrida's own stepdaughter, St Edith of Wilton, making a great show of her rank through dress while in her convent, for example. According to the Life of St Edith, Ethelwold, Bishop of Winchester (the former Abbot of Abingdon), once upbraided her on her clothes, considering them unbecoming to a woman living in a convent.[22] To this, Edith responded that 'a mind by no means poorer in aspiring to God will live beneath a goatskin. I possess my Lord, who pays attention to the mind, not to the clothing.' Edith was proved correct when a serving girl dropped a lit candle into one of her many chests of clothes, causing it to burn all night. When the accident was discovered, Edith's fine furs and clothes of imperial purple were found to be unharmed.[23]

Fine golden clothes were clearly considered to be appropriate to a king's daughter even if, in Edith's case, she reputedly wore a hair shirt for pious reasons under her finery.[24] Although no description survives of Elfrida, she is likely to have decked herself out in something similar to befit her status as queen. She was acutely conscious of her status as Edgar's legitimate wife and would certainly not have allowed herself to be overshadowed by her stepdaughter, the daughter of her rejected predecessor and a woman whom she appears to have disliked. Edgar's previous wife, Wulfthryth, is known to have worn 'gold-embroidered purple' during her marriage, as well as gold jewellery, and it is safe to assume that Elfrida would have been similarly attired when participating in court ceremonies.[25] Similarly, Wulfthryth is also supposed to have abandoned 'golden garlands, gold-embroidered cloaks, bejewelled purple, bracelets, rings, necklaces and the varied splendour of ornamental ornaments' when she became a nun, perhaps even leaving them for her successor to appropriate.[26] The ex-wife of Eadwig, Elfgifu, left armlets, a necklace and a headband, items that are likely to have been particularly fine, since they were mentioned in her Will.[27] Similarly, another former queen, Ethelflaed of Damerham, bequeathed four robes, which again must have been fine enough to merit special mention. Edgar's maternal grandmother, Wynflaed, if indeed she can be identified as the tenth-century testatrix of the same name, left an engraved bracelet and brooch, gowns, a cap and headband, as well as other linen.[28]

There is evidence that, in the Anglo-Saxon period, the queen bore the responsibility for ensuring that the king and court looked sufficiently regal. According to the Life of King Edward who Rests at Westminster, Elfrida's own grandson, Edward the Confessor, showed little interest in the trappings of royalty and spent much of his time hunting and hawking.[29] His wife, Edith, prided herself on taking him in hand and providing him with rich clothes and a throne draped in gold fabrics. She also purchased Spanish carpets for the floor, something that would have been almost unheard of in England. As queen, Elfrida would also have been responsible for helping to ensure that the court materially reflected the king's status.

Although there is evidence that Elfrida spent much time at court, her everyday activities are less well known. Her stepdaughter, Edith, is known to have painted, as well as to have written prayers of her own composition.[30] Elfrida may also have taken part in such activities. More certainly, she would have known how to sew and to embroider, a skill that a royal woman was expected to employ for the benefit of the Church. Princess Edith made a particularly splendid vestment for the church at Wilton, with her biographer reminiscing that

> she embroidered with flowers the pontifical vestments of Christ with all her skill and capacity to make splendid. Here purple, dyed with Punic red, with murex and Sidonian shellfish, and twice-dipped scarlet were interwoven with gold; chrysolite, topaz, onyx and beryl and precious stones were intertwined with gold; union pearls, the shells' treasure, which only India produces in the east and Britain, the land of the English, in the west, were set like stars in gold; the golden insignia of the cross, the golden image of the saints were outlined with a surround of pearls.[31]

As the queen, Elfrida worked with only the finest materials, and her embroidery work, which occupied much of her time, would have been sumptuous. Most likely, her work adorned the church, as did that of her daughter-in-law, Emma, who provided a number of embroidered items for the monastery at Ely, decorated with gold and silver.[32] This included a pall for the tomb of St Ethelthryth, decorated in gold and jewels, which was 'an offering which Queen Emma had presented, to be a covering for the tomb of the holy virgin'.[33] Perhaps it was Elfrida who made an alb from the boots of King Edgar, which was still a treasured possession of the monastery at Ely in the twelfth century. Alternatively, she may have been responsible for converting a rich cloak of Edgar's, made of purpura (a rich and shining type of cloth), and embroidered with gold, into a chasuble for the monastery.[34] Her predecessor as queen, Elfflaed, the second wife of Edward the Elder, certainly seems to have been involved in tapestry-work for the relics of St Cuthbert.

It is clear that a royal woman in the late tenth century was able to live in some comfort. Princess Edith possessed a 'cauldron in which her bath was heated', for example, a 'mod con' that her stepmother could have acquired if she wished.[35] Edith also kept her own private zoo at Wilton, another diversion available to the highest status women.[36] She spent so much time with her exotic and native animals that many would eat out of her hand.

Although Elfrida was often at court, she also employed her own household of officials and servants, with a large retinue that would, to some extent, mirror the king's. Becoming a member of the queen's household could be very lucrative, and a stepping-stone to a grand career. When Elfrida's daughter-in-law, Emma of Normandy, arrived in England, she was accompanied by a large number of her countrymen, as the twelfth-century chronicler, Orderic Vitallis, made clear in his comments regarding the marriage of the daughter of Henry I:

> Burchard, bishop of Cambrai, received her from her father and escorted her to her husband. Roger, son of Richard and many other Normans also accompanied her, expecting through this marriage to climb to an influential position in the empire, and hoping eventually to win the highest rank for themselves by their daring or ruthlessness. This was the way their ancestors had won power in England through Emma, Duke Richard's daughter.[37]

Emma's followers made up her household and provided for the administration of her lands. Although little evidence of them survives today, one member of her establishment can be glimpsed in the Anglo-Saxon Chronicle's record for 1003, which complained that Exeter was captured by the Vikings due to the treachery of Emma's reeve, a Frenchman called Hugh.[38]

Elfrida, while not a foreign-born queen, would have brought some of her own servants from her home to serve her. The queen's household could be substantial: it has been calculated that around seventy to eighty people can be associated with Edith Godwin in the Domesday Book.[39] These followers were mainly made up of the nobility, and it was clearly an honour to serve the queen. Some household members were employed to take care of the queen's intimate needs, including chaplains, stewards and maids. Edgar's grandmother, Wynflaed, had a serf to act as her seamstress.[40] Elfrida would not have required the services of a 'sword-polisher' as her grandson later did, but she may have employed a seneschal and even a stag huntsman, which are recorded in this grandson's Will.[41] These are the people with whom the queen lived on a daily basis. Elfrida's household provided her with company and entertainment when she was apart from the king, and was probably made up of some of her most important supporters. She provided advancement and preferment for them and, in return, they offered her tangible support in crises such as the succession dispute of 975.

Not all of the people associated with Elfrida would have been members of her household, with many employed in the administration of her lands. Anglo-Saxon queens were wealthy and needed a large retinue of people to effectively administer these estates. Edith Godwin, for example, possessed over 1,000 hides in the Domesday Book, making her one of the wealthiest people in England and, certainly, the wealthiest woman.[42] Landed wealth was an important part of Anglo-Saxon queenship and, although less evidence survives for her than the wife of her grandson, some evidence of Elfrida's wealth can also be seen. She inherited lands from her first husband too, which were at least sufficient to allow her to provide for her stepdaughter, Ethelflaed, and her gifts to Romsey Abbey. Claims that she was an heiress suggest that she was promised a substantial share of her father's booklands on his death. She is certainly known to have owned a house at Corfe in Dorset by the 970s and, given its location, this may well have come to her from her father.

The earliest queens of Wessex were granted little land, as befitted their low status. Alfred the Great's wife, Eahlswith, for example, seems to have only possessed a few rural estates in Berkshire and Wiltshire, and a property in Winchester, hardly enough to make her a great landowner.[43] This may have been part of the general policy to keep queens in the background, as land ownership was a route to political power – something Eadgifu, an heiress, was able to exploit. In a statement about some of her inherited land in Kent that Eadgifu made during the reign of King Edgar, she made it clear just how in control of her own affairs she was. According to Eadgifu, her father, Ealdorman Sigelm, had redeemed some land that he had mortgaged to a man named Goda shortly before his death in battle.[44] Sigelm left the land, and other property, to Eadgifu, something that was certainly behind the elderly Edward the Elder's decision to divorce his wife and marry Eadgifu. With Sigelm dead, Goda refused to hand over the land, claiming that the money had not been paid. According to Eadgifu herself, it took her six long years of petitioning the influential men of the kingdom to win her case, finally making a personal oath before the royal council at Aylesford to clear her father of the suspicion of the debt, and 'even then she could not get possession of the estate until her friends induced King Edward to declare that Goda must restore the estate, if he wished to hold any land at all, and so he relinquished it'. It was Eadgifu's persistence and political influence that won the case for her. In her son Eadred's Will, she was also bequeathed a large landholding spread across England.[45] Although this is not evidence of an actual dower, this large landholding would have set a precedent for later queens and also provided Eadgifu with an independent authority. The power it gave her is evident from the fact that Eadwig deprived his grandmother of her lands as a means of politically neutralising her.

Edgar's stepmother, Ethelflaed of Damerhan, who was accorded the title of queen in her lifetime, was also an heiress; her father, Ealdorman Elfgar, made large bequests of land to her in his Will.[46] That Ethelflaed was able to assert her full control over the estates is clear from her own Will, made after she had been widowed for a second time, and some time after Edgar's death.[47] Some of her bequests were even of questionable legality. For example, an estate at Cockfield, left to her by her father for her lifetime with the remainder to a monastery, was bequeathed to Ethelflaed's sister and brother-in-law in her own Will for the duration of their lives before it reverted to the Church. In her Will Ethelflaed also made a bequest to the king (either Edward the Martyr or Ethelred II), granting him her estates at Lambourn, Cholsey and Reading as well as some moveable property; this may, perhaps, have been the return of her dower.[48] The Will of another royal wife, that of Elfgifu, the divorced spouse of Eadwig, contained a similar bequest, passing estates at Wing, Linslade, Haversham, Hatfield, Masworth and Gussage to Edgar.[49] Ethelflaed of Damerham, Elfgifu and Edgar's first wife, Ethelflaed *Eneda*, all had a connection with Hatfield, for example, perhaps suggesting that the estate had a connection with queenly dowers in the ninth century.[50]

Edith Godwin's lands were spread across the country and this would have made the queen influential in a number of areas. A particular association with Rutland can be seen in hers and later queens dowers, something that is first identifiable with Elfrida, who is the first English queen known to have received a dower on her marriage.[51] In Elfrida's case, this was land at Aston Upthorpe following her marriage to Edgar – an attempt to provide her with the wealth deemed appropriate to a queen.[52] She also received an estate near Blewbury in Berkshire in a charter that was witnessed by her father.[53] This was, in fact, the last time that Ordgar witnessed as a thegn, being appointed as ealdorman of Devon soon afterwards – an appointment certainly attributable to the marriage of his daughter. More grants to Elfrida are also likely to have been made around the time of her marriage. Gaimar believed that Elfrida was granted property in Winchester, the capital, on her marriage, as well as estates in Rockingham and Rutland, lands that later passed to her successor as queen, Emma of Normandy.[54] Marriage gifts, even for those below a queen, could be substantial, with the sister of Ethelflaed of Damerham recording in her Will that she had received an estate on her marriage to an ealdorman.[55] The queen could, of course, expect to do somewhat better on marrying the king.

Land gave a queen political power, as Elfrida had witnessed from Eadgifu. Like her husband's grandmother, Elfrida was determined to use this power, and she is remembered as a major influence on the king during the greatest achievement of his reign: the tenth-century religious reform.

5

THE TENTH-CENTURY RELIGIOUS REFORM

Edgar's reign is remembered primarily for the religious reform that it ushered in. No study of Elfrida would be complete without a discussion of the major role that she played in the reform movement. Her devotion to the cause eclipsed even the pious Queen Eadgifu, although both women were able to use their religious patronage politically, as King Edgar himself did. In many respects, the origins of Elfrida's establishment as queen can be seen in her willingness to play a major role in the reform itself.

By the early tenth century, the Church in England was in a ruinous state. The Viking attacks of the ninth century had nearly destroyed the church in some areas and a number of previously great bishoprics in Northumbria and East Anglia had fallen into abeyance.[1] The see of Dunwich, for example, ceased to exist around 870 and was never revived.[2] Elmham also disappeared around 836, although it was revived a century later. The great Northern see of York was so impoverished that many of its archbishops found it necessary to hold the wealthy see of Worcester at the same time in order to support themselves. Other sees, such as Leicester, were forced to move to less vulnerable positions in the face of the Viking onslaught.

Alfred the Great noted this decline in the late ninth century, but was, apparently, powerless to remedy the situation. His son, Edward the Elder, founded the New Minster at Winchester in the early tenth century and Alfred's widow, Eahlswith, also founded Nunnaminster in the same city.[3] This failed to staunch the decline however, with contemporary criticism centring on the lack of discipline in the religious houses that still survived.[4] Few monks remained in England and the monasteries were instead filled with secular clerks, who did not abide by any monastic rule. Many of the clergy were married and it was difficult to distinguish them from their congregations in their parishes.[5] Most worryingly for the tenth-century reformers, the Rule of St Benedict had not taken hold in the religious houses. This was a central rule through which monks and nuns could order their lives. Elfrida was born at a time when the Church in England was in a deprived state and, with clear evidence that her family were interested in reform, it is no surprise that she took a keen interest in the movement which began to gain momentum during the reign of Edward the Elder's eldest son, Athelstan.

King Athelstan was interested in the reform movement, although it appears to have made little progress in England during his reign. Two of the most prominent reformers, Dunstan and Ethelwold, were, however, educated at his court and were first exposed to the ideals of the reform there.[6] Athelstan was also responsible for the appointment of Oda as Archbishop of Canterbury in 942, a man who had formerly been a monk at the reformed continental house at Fleury.[7] Until his death in 958 Oda consistently promoted reform in England, handing over the mantle to younger men shortly before Edgar came to the throne.

The reform movement first developed in Continental Europe. As in England, churches had been badly damaged by the Vikings and, around 910, a movement began at Cluny in Burgundy to return to an idealised view of earlier monasticism.[8] These ideas quickly spread and had reached Fleury by the time that Oda was there. The ideals of the reform obviously caught his imagination, and his nephew, Oswald, on his uncle's advice, was also to study there, bringing the latest ideas relating to reform home with him.[9]

It was in this context that Edgar was fostered by the reform-minded Athelstan Half-King in the 940s, later finishing his education under Abbot Ethelwold at Abingdon, the most zealous of all the English reformers. Ethelwold set about instilling the ideals of the reform into his pupil, securing a promise from him that, when king, he would advance the cause of Abingdon.[10] Ethelwold's admonishments took the form of explaining to his young pupil the plight of the monasteries and how they desperately needed reform.[11] He informed the prince that 'there were only a few monks in a few places in so large a kingdom who lived by the right rule'.[12] This was a subject close to Ethelwold's own heart, and Edgar was seen as the hope of the reformers. St Dunstan also took an interest in Edgar's future, for which he was well rewarded.

St Dunstan is widely held to have been the leader of the reform movement in England and, certainly, he was the most prominent. He was born around 909 and joined the household of his uncle, Ethelhelm, Archbishop of Canterbury, as a youth.[13] He was related to King Athelstan through the king's mother, Ecgwyna, something that helped him rise as a member of the king's court. Dunstan was always intended for the Church and, around 936, he became a monk.[14] His close association with the royal family meant that, around 940, he was created Abbot of Glastonbury by Athelstan's successor, King Edmund. Dunstan decided to implement the Continental religious reform at his monastery and spent the next fifteen years ensuring that Glastonbury reached his own high standards, for example by ensuring that the monks ate in a common refectory and slept in a dormitory.[15] He barred married men from being admitted, in a direct challenge to the secular clerks who inhabited most of the other monasteries in England.

As well as involving himself with Glastonbury, Dunstan was also a courtier, spending a considerable amount of time at both Edmund and Eadred's courts. He was a leading advisor to the sickly Eadred, whose death was a major setback for Dunstan. Unlike Ethelwold, Dunstan quickly fell out of favour with Eadwig, with the pair's relationship dissolving into outright hostility as early as the coronation banquet, with the churchman later being exiled to Flanders. As already discussed, Eadwig's opposition to Dunstan and his grandmother, Eadgifu, did not necessarily mean that he was opposed to the religious reform. In all probability, much of the later hostility towards Eadwig and his wife, who is usually called a concubine by later writers, emanated from Dunstan, since it is clear that the young king was on friendly terms with Abbot Ethelwold. Dunstan had backed Edgar as king, following Eadred's death, perhaps due to his reformist upbringing, and claims that he had heard an angelic voice proclaiming peace at the time that Edgar was born[16] cannot have helped his position with the new king.

Dunstan's support of Edgar later paid off and, following the partition of the kingdom, he was recalled by Edgar to become Bishop of Worcester.[17] What Edgar made of the character of his new bishop is not clear, but he probably realised that he needed

Dunstan's support if he was to aspire to the throne of England itself. The bishop was a driven and self-righteous character and must have been a difficult man for a king to have at court. William of Malmesbury refers to him as a denouncer of kings and princes who transgressed.[18] He had little respect for Eadwig, manhandling the king when he left his coronation banquet early. He was also rumoured (probably incorrectly) to have imposed a penance on Edgar for carrying off a nun.[19] As well as policing the kings under whom he served, Dunstan took a keen interest in the morals of Edgar's subjects and is recorded as having invented a peg to be fastened to communal drinking pots to ensure that no man could drink more than his fair share.[20] Edgar's upbringing may have predisposed him to overlook Dunstan's more domineering character traits, since he was a firm favourite of his foster father, the Half-King. Elfrida, on the other hand, took the view of her brother-in-law, Eadwig, and she and Dunstan loathed each other, in spite of their common interest in reform. By the time of her marriage, he and Edgar had already ousted Eadwig's candidate for Archbishop of Canterbury, who had been hastily appointed following Oda's death, with Dunstan instead taking the primacy of the Church in England. This may, in fact, account for some of the hostility between Dunstan and Elfrida, since the ousted archbishop, Brihtelm, had previously been Bishop of Dorset, a position for which he would have required the support of her father, Ordgar. An angry and humiliated Brihtelm was forced to return to his original see in 959, no doubt complaining loudly to his patron about his treatment.

Dunstan proved to be an enthusiastic archbishop and, according to William of Malmesbury, he quickly became Edgar's chief counsellor:

The divine spirit had assuredly breathed on the heart of the king, for he looked to Dunstan's advice in all matters and unhesitatingly did whatever the archbishop was minded to command. For his part Dunstan never left out what he knew was consonant with the king's reputation and safety. When the king hesitated, he would put sharper pressure on him. Whenever he transgressed, Dunstan pointed to his own previous way of life as a model for his subjects, and he would mete out savage punishments without any respect of persons.[21]

For all his power, however, as the leader of the reform movement, it was Dunstan's former pupil, Ethelwold, who pursued it with the greatest zeal.

Ethelwold was of noble birth and an almost exact contemporary of Dunstan. He entered the service of King Athelstan as an adolescent and it was the king himself who recommended that he become a monk.[22] Ethelwold and Dunstan were ordained on the same day by the Bishop of Winchester, although it was the latter, with his stronger royal connections, who rose more quickly: not long after his ordination Ethelwold entered Dunstan's monastery at Glastonbury as an ordinary monk.[23] Ethelwold thrived under the Rule of St Benedict, and it is some measure of his austere character that he soon came to feel Glastonbury was not strict enough for him. By the mid-940s he had decided to leave England for a Continental religious house, only to be thwarted in this wish when the king's mother, Eadgifu, who had identified him as an up-and-coming young churchman, persuaded Eadred to forbid him to leave.[24]

Ethelwold may well have been disappointed with Eadgifu's action and, throughout his later life, he showed a fascination with the Continental monasteries. His disappointment was mitigated by his appointment by Eadred, also on Eadgifu's advice, to the position of Abbot of Abingdon, allowing him the opportunity to create a house according to his own austere tastes.[25] Eadgifu, who remembered Ethelwold from his earlier court career, was a particular supporter and she 'cherished the abbot and monks with the greatest love. Sometimes she showered quantities of her wealth on them, at other times she sought her son's favour for them by assiduous persuasions'.[26] Both she and her son, the king, loaded the new abbey with financial aid, something that it badly needed.

For Ethelwold, his first visit to Abingdon must have been a shock, having come from the wealthy Glastonbury. Abingdon had been a monastery for several centuries but, by the mid-940s, it was neglected, with ruined buildings and an endowment of only forty hides of land.[27] Its new abbot quickly set about trying to improve his new home, taking some monks with him from Glastonbury in order to promulgate his Benedictine rule.[28] At the same time, Eadred provided Abingdon with a more substantial endowment, giving Ethelwold one hundred hides of royal land and money at the time of his appointment.[29] This grant greatly increased Abingdon's prestige, as did the lavish gifts that Eadgifu showered on her protégé and his new monastery.

For Ethelwold, this may have been the moment when he realised the advantages of gaining the favour of the queen and it was a policy that he followed for the rest of his life. He also remained in favour with the king, even during Eadwig's reign, something that demonstrates he could be considerably more diplomatic than Dunstan when circumstances demanded. Whether he was personally liked by his young pupil, Edgar, is less certain, given that it took some time for the king to supply him with a bishopric during his reign, when they were quickly provided for other leading churchmen. However, Edgar certainly respected him and he was on very good terms with Elfrida. She was reputed to be so close to the churchman that she was able to hide one day in his cupboard, in order to listen to his prays so that she could learn of some way to help him.[30] As he knelt to pray, she stood still in her hiding place and listened closely to him request to be allowed to refound Peterborough Abbey according to the Rule of St Benedict. As soon as she had heard this, Elfrida leapt out of the cupboard, promising to persuade Edgar to agree to Ethelwold's request, before immediately going to achieve just that. Whether true or not, the story shows the high level of access that the queen and the bishop had to each other. Peterborough was evidently particularly coveted by Ethelwold and, following its acquisition (with Elfrida's aid), he loaded it with material wealth, including providing a gospel book adorned with silver, three silver cross, candlesticks of gold and silver, rich vestments and soft furnishings, all intended to display the glory of his new monastery.[31]

Ethelwold was still Abbot of Abingdon at the time of Edgar's accession, and he remained connected to the monastery throughout his life. He spent the bulk of his time at court during the early years of Edgar's reign, joining the king's service as a clerk and advisor, something that was a natural appointment by a former pupil. In 963 Ethelwold reached the height of his prestige, becoming Bishop of Winchester.[32]

Although Dunstan and Ethelwold were the most well-known of the tenth-century reformers, there was a third great reforming churchman who came to prominence under Edgar, securing his bishopric even before Ethelwold, when he was appointed as Bishop of Worcester on Dunstan's recommendation.[33] Archbishop Oda had encouraged his nephew Oswald to study at Fleury during his youth, intending him for high office in the Church. Oswald appears in the sources as a more attractive figure than Ethelwold and, although he was devoted to the Rule of St Benedict, did not seek to enforce its observance as harshly.[34] He was in high favour throughout the reign and, in 972, was appointed Archbishop of York, the second-highest Church position in England.[35]

Dunstan, Ethelwold and Oswald are remembered as the main tenth-century reformers, and they accomplished a great deal in their reform of the Church. They could not have done so, however, without the support of King Edgar and the English queens, Eadgifu and Elfrida. The monastic reformers relied on royal patronage to accomplish their aims and, in the main, it was the royal women who responded to their appeals.[36] Had Elfrida's reputation not become overshadowed by the murder of Edward the Martyr, she would almost certainly be remembered as a great religious queen in the same vein as her grandmother-in-law, Eadgifu.

For Elfrida, the roots of this interest probably lay in her childhood. Following his elevation to the rank of ealdorman, her father, Ordgar, had authority over the whole of Devon and Cornwall. In 968 the monastery at Exeter was refounded, a process in which Ordgar was almost certainly involved, given that he was buried there a few years later.[37] He is sometimes erroneously given as the founder of Tavistock Abbey, although that honour in fact belongs to his son, Ordulf. Tavistock was a particularly attractive house for monks to join since, according to William of Malmesbury, it lay 'in a lovely spot with woods near by and a plentiful supply of fish. The material of the church matches its surroundings, and streams from the river flow in between the outbuildings of the monks and under the rush of their own impetus carry away all the rubbish they find in their path.'[38] Ordulf also patronised another monastery at Horton in Dorset and he was considered to be an influential founder by both monasteries. According to William of Malmesbury, the two monasteries competed for his body after his death, with the Abbot of Tavistock carrying off the corpse for his own monastery.[39] Ordulf's wife, Abina, was similarly interested in reform, being listed as one of the benefactors of Tavistock.[40]

Elfrida herself took a keen interest in the foundation of her brother's monastery. When it was finally ready for its foundation charter in 981 she attended the council at which it was granted, with both she and her son, King Ethelred, confirming the donation; their consent was presumably required to ensure that, as the descendants of Ordgar, they later made no challenge to Ordulf's gifts. Elfrida's first marriage to the son of the reform-minded Half-King also supports the view that such ideas were already current in her own family, as does her early patronage of Romsey and the dedication of her stepdaughter to the nunnery there. Elfrida was later to found two nunneries of her own and it is in regard to religious houses for women that she was able to play the strongest role in relation to the reform, whether their occupants liked it or not.

6

ELFRIDA'S ROLE IN THE REFORM MOVEMENT

The accession of Edgar and the appointments of Dunstan, Ethelwold and Oswald as bishops ushered in the most intense phase of the tenth-century religious reform, and Elfrida was intimately involved with many aspects of it.

Even before her marriage to the king, Elfrida was able to influence him in relation to the religious reform movement since, according to the *Liber Eliensis*,

> a woman called Aelfthryth [Elfrida] pleaded with King Edgar that he sell to the blessed Aethelwold ten hides at Stoke, which is near Ipswich; and two mills which are situated in the southern part. Her entreaties availed with him. For the bishop gave the king one hundred mancuses for that land and the mills, [and] he afterwards presented [the same land and mills] to St Aethelthryth.[1]

Given Edgar's ready acquiescence to Elfrida's demands, it would seem likely that the pair were already intending to marry – perhaps only waiting for Wulfthryth's retirement to Wilton. Given that it was Ethelwold himself who made the arrangements for Wulfthryth's repudiation, it is interesting that he was already associated with Elfrida before her marriage, something suggesting that the pair were already associated politically, perhaps having made each other's acquaintance during Elfrida's first marriage. Could it be that Ethelwold was influential in first drawing Elfrida's attention to her future husband, the king, knowing that she was a woman who would support his own views on religious reform?

Much of Elfrida's interest in religious reform certainly centred on the advancement of Ethelwold, whom she counted as a personal friend and later lamented after his death, and the bishop must have known that he could always rely on the queen to advance his interests at court. She may have been aware that Ethelwold intended to donate the land to Ely, a monastery that was close to her first husband's base, and which she is likely to have been familiar with through him. Certainly, she often gave generously to the house, for example jointly giving land at Marsworth in Buckinghamshire to Ely with King Edgar after their marriage.[2] Both Edgar and Elfrida were genuinely pious, something they shared with the majority of their contemporaries: the account in the *Liber Eliensis* of Edgar's stepmother, Ethelflaed of Damerham, who 'frequently sought out our [Ely's] saints with heartfelt love and veneration, and devoutly used to attend vigils at their shrines' would have been familiar to them, with the near-contemporary Life of St Oswald also speaking of Edgar's piety at an Easter court when he encouraged all of his attendants to attend mass.

Ethelwold's appointment as Bishop of Winchester in 963 provided him with a position from which he could implement his reformist ideals in the centre of the kingdom of Wessex. He launched into this with gusto and, according to the Anglo-Saxon Chronicle, in the next year after he was consecrated he founded many monasteries, and drove the clerks out of the bishopric because they would not observe any rule, and set monks there. He founded there two abbacies, one of monks the other of nuns – that was all inside Winchester. Then afterwards he came to King Edgar [and] asked him that he would give him all the monasteries the heathen men had broken up earlier, because he wanted to restore it; and the king happily granted it.[3]

Ethelwold moved quickly in instigating the reform in his bishopric, and was determined to bring the English monasteries into line with the Continent and to ensure that they observed the Rule of St Benedict. Thwarted in his own attempts to view Continental monasticism first-hand, he sent one of his monks from Abingdon, Osgar, to Fleury to observe the Rule and report back to him on its details.[4] He was also in direct contact with the Continental monasteries. Eager to learn the correct form of the Rule of St Benedict, Ethelwold persuaded the Abbot of Corbie in France to send over a group of monks to teach his monks Gregorian chants.[5] These contacts with the Continental monasteries led to Ethelwold being considered as the pre-eminent authority on the Rule of St Benedict in England, with Edgar and Elfrida jointly commissioning an English translation of the Rule from the bishop, providing him with an estate at Sudbourne for his labours, which he promptly donated to the monastery at Ely.[6] The couple liked what they read and, within a few years of their marriage, Edgar called a council at Winchester to discuss the monastic rule.

This council at Winchester is famous for the document it produced, the *Regularis Concordia*, and it appears to have been the first great council to have religious reform as its central theme. Edgar summoned all his leading secular nobles and churchmen to the council and it must have been a grand affair, with Elfrida almost certainly in attendance. She is unlikely to have accepted any order that she be excluded from such an important event, and she must have been eager to lend her support to Ethelwold's party at the meeting. Certainly, the bishop himself would have insisted on her presence at the council and the office of queen, which Elfrida embodied, was central to his views on how the Church should be reformed.

The *Regularis Concordia* is essentially a statement giving the point of view of the reformers and sets out the rule by which they expected monks and nuns to live. Dunstan is known to have played a role in deciding the rule at the council,[7] however it was Ethelwold who drafted the document and it is his view that shines through above all others. Ethelwold sought to repay Elfrida's devotion to him, and the *Regularis Concordia* is remarkable in its focus on the role of the queen. There is no doubt that this position benefited both the queen and the bishop, providing the royal consort with a specified political role for the first time in English history.

The *Regularis Concordia* gave Edgar, as the king, control over all the monks in England in order to ensure that they did not fall under the control of secular lords. This, in itself, was a major change to religion in England, but Ethelwold, in his document, went further, adding,

And he [Edgar] saw to it wisely that his queen Aelfthryth [Elfrida], should be the protectress and fearless guardian of the monasteries; so that he himself helping the men and his consort helping the women there should be no cause for any breath of scandal.[8]

Given Edgar's reputation regarding nunneries it is understandable that he agreed to relinquish direct control of the nuns in order to avoid scandal. However, the choice of Elfrida as the protector of the nunneries is striking. Even the powerful Eadgifu never had a defined political role, for all her gifts to the Church. It was, therefore, in no way inevitable that Elfrida would be placed at the head of the nunneries and her appointment must be linked to her own personal capabilities. It must also be set in the context of her relationship with Bishop Ethelwold, something that was mutually beneficial to both, and he demanded that the queen should be of enhanced political status.

The *Regularis Concordis* was not the only document Ethelwold had a hand in that emphasised the important religious role of a queen. In the medieval period parallels were commonly drawn between an earthly queen and Mary, the Queen of Heaven,[9] and this was something Ethelwold also sought to promote. The *Benedictional of St Aethelwold*, which is one of the most lavishly decorated surviving Anglo-Saxon manuscripts, and which was commissioned by Ethelwold for his personal use, contains one of the earliest known representations of the coronation of the Virgin in English art, an inclusion that is telling in relation to Ethelwold's own relationship with Elfrida.[10] The Benedictional was produced by a monk named Godeman,[11] who was an associate of Ethelwold's and who is likely to have seen Elfrida: it therefore seems not impossible that the representation of the Virgin in the Benedictional might just be based on an earthly queen, providing the only surviving contemporary image of Elfrida.

According to the *Regularis Concordia*, at the council Dunstan added further instructions on how the houses of monks and nuns were to be run, declaring that no monk, nor indeed any man whatever his rank, should dare to enter and frequent the places set apart for nuns; and that those who have spiritual authority over nuns should use their powers not as worldly tyrants but in the interests of good discipline.[12]

This decree ensured that the monks and nuns were kept separate and that the nunneries remained a distinctly female sphere. At first glance, this could be said to have been a limit to Elfrida's power, keeping it confined to a marginal side of religion. However, there is no doubt that this decree also helped Elfrida develop and consolidate her own power base. By not allowing men to enter the nunneries, this decree removed the practical power of either the king or the bishops over the nunneries. They were unable to enter and, so, also unable to see first-hand the workings of the nunneries, instead they had to rely on the experiences of others, such as the queen. The *Regularis Concordia* itself states that the election of abbots and abbesses could only be carried out with the consent and advice of the king.[13] Edgar would probably use the advice of his senior bishops, as well as his own experiences of the monasteries, to make his decision in the appointment of any new abbots. However, when it came to the appointment of abbesses, assuming that he was to have no further ex-wives to dispose of, Edgar is likely to have turned for advice to others. Since Elfrida was bound by the Rule to take an interest in the nunneries anyway, it seems only natural that the person that the king turned to was his own wife. It is very likely that it was Elfrida who advised Edgar on the appointment of abbesses and other matters concerning the nunneries, providing her with a power base that other members of Edgar's government could not challenge. This would certainly account for much of the virulent hostility which seems to have been directed towards her from many of the nunneries in England.

As the head of the nunneries in England, Elfrida's role was a somewhat fluid one and open to her own interpretation. It has been noted that, in the Anglo-Saxon period, the presence of women in the Church was particularly unstable.[14] While monasticism, in its earliest English form, was exclusively for men, nuns and nunneries had become prominent by the ninth century, with a number of very influential royal women serving as abbesses. The nunneries were, however, as susceptible to Viking attacks as houses for men; at least forty-one nunneries were destroyed by the ninth century, with very few remaining.[15] The Vikings were often particularly ferocious when confronted with women; the nuns of Barking Abbey, which was destroyed in 870, were burned alive within the confines of their house. Barking itself was not revived until the monastery was handed to Wulfhild, the kinswoman of Wulfthryth, after Edgar finally accepted that she meant to refuse him.

By the time of Edgar's council at Winchester when the *Regularis Concordia* was produced, some nunneries remained or had been re-established, and some abbesses and nuns were prominent enough to attend the council themselves. However, the role of the nuns was never paramount in the minds of the reformers, with only six or seven new nunneries created in England in the period. It is certainly true that nuns were not particularly high on Ethelwold's agenda, with a number of former nunneries or joint houses, such as Ely, being refounded in the period as houses exclusively for men. However, while Ethelwold and his fellow reformers had little interest in the nuns, the fact that they were prepared to hand control of what houses there were to Elfrida had the potential to accord her with a good deal of power: if no one else in authority was particularly interested in the houses then they were, largely, Elfrida's domain. By the end of her life she had established two nunneries of her own (Wherwell and Amesbury), as well as dedicating her stepdaughter and giving generously to Romsey, thus clearly showing a deep and lasting interest in female monasticism absent from most of the other reformers of the period. In this sense, as well as with her other religious interests, it is clear that Elfrida was a major mover in the tenth-century religious reform and should be considered one of the people most strongly involved in the continuation of female monasticism and its reform in England. This is particularly vivid given that many of Elfrida's female contemporaries and later medieval women chose to support male houses rather than female.[16]

Elfrida's pre-eminence was not accepted in the nunneries without considerable challenge, and it has been noted that the most scurrilous stories surrounding her seem to have emanated from them. On a personal level, her movement into the female religious sphere stepped on the toes of her predecessor, Wulfthryth, who had given up her position as queen in return for the role of an abbess. Wilton, Wulfthryth's nunnery, was the wealthiest and most important in England and there is evidence that Elfrida faced a challenge to her authority from her predecessor and, towards the end of Edgar's reign, from her stepdaughter. Edith, who, with her 'reddish hair' closely resembled her father.[17] She proved to be a favourite of his, enjoyed considerable influence with her father, even from within her nunnery. The king employed two Continental scholars to be her tutors, a move intended to ensure that she was well versed in the tenets of the religious reform.[18] The plan appears to have been that Edith would become an abbess, being consecrated as head of three nunneries, including Nunnaminster in Winchester.[19] These appointments, alongside Wulfthryth's position as head of Wilton, and their kinswoman Wulfhild first at Barking and then at Horton, meant that the party of the king's former wife was in control of a large swathe of the English nunneries, something that can only have made Elfrida's task more difficult. It was perhaps due to her influence that Edith failed to take active control of any of her appointments, remaining with her mother at Wilton. She was certainly behind the driving out of Wulfhild from Barking Abbey after Edgar's death for failure to comply with the Rule.

Wulfthryth, in particular, clashed with Bishop Ethelwold during her time as abbess, presumably resenting his interference into her domain. In the eleventh-century Life of her daughter, for example, which was written very close to the living memory of both Wulfthryth and Edith, it was recalled at Wilton that the abbess had come into conflict with the bishop when he had attempted to obtain a piece of one of the nails from the cross, a relic that Wulfthryth had herself obtained through her own funds and endeavours from a Continental house. The Life declared that 'the reverend Ethelwold, inflamed with holy avarice, involved himself with this token of grace, eager to take up what he had not laid down to reap what he had not sowed'.[20] Ethelwold's involvement in Wulfthryth's divorce and his championing of Elfrida may well be behind this negative portrayal, with Elfrida similarly smeared in the work. A recent study has concluded that Wilton cannot be shown to have been reformed during Wulfthryth's time as abbess,[21] something that is a testament to her pre-eminence there and what must have been, for Elfrida, a frustrating example of the limits on her power over the nunneries. The presence of her stepdaughter must always have been a concern to Elfrida, given her father's indulgent devotion. Edith was known to have considerable influence with him; the Life of Edith recorded,

> Whatever she demanded from her pious father by delegates or by her own speaking, this was in her heart – that he should increase the number of churches, support them with riches, extend the embrace of his mercy to all needs, and set free by his clemency those who were to be punished or sold into slavery. Her piety and concern did not seek any gifts for herself, but the well being of others. Nor was it difficult to obtain her requests from the indulgence of that father, whose throne had been prepared on mercy, whose judgement preferred to pardon rather than to punish (provided only the people's peace was preserved), so that the grace of his daughter would put aside his sword, even when it had been drawn.[22]

Edith's political activities, which can only have begun to become manifest towards the end of the reign, led to Elfrida and her stepdaughter vying for the role of principal woman in the religious reform movement.

By limiting the power that secular benefactors had over monasteries, the *Regularis Concordia* also helped increase Elfrida's prominence as queen. The council forbade secular lords to hold monasteries as their personal possessions, and ordered the bishops to live with their monks in order to monitor and inspire them.[23] This secular lordship was also to be replaced by the dominance of the king and queen, again highlighting the importance of Elfrida's role. According to the text, they [the council] commanded that the sovereign power of the king and queen – and that only – should ever be besought with confidant petition, both for the safeguarding of the holy places and for the increase of the goods of the church. As often therefore as it shall be to their advantage the fathers and mothers of each house shall have humble access to the king and queen in the fear of God and observance of the Rule.[24]

Head of the nunneries was clearly meant to be no empty title and Elfrida showed a genuine interest in this position, due both to her interest in the reform, and for the possibilities of safeguarding her queenship that it offered. The actual text of the Rule in the *Regularis Concordia* also makes it clear that the king and queen were expected to be an integral part of monastic life, both being central and almost taking the form of a dual monarchy with regard to monasticism and the Church. Throughout the day, the Rule decreed that psalms would be said for the king, queen and any benefactors of the house.[25] This would ensure both that Edgar and Elfrida were constantly in the minds of the monks and nuns and that they were firmly associated with the religious reform and its emphasis of a return to a holier past.

Much of Elfrida's personal patronage was centred on her support for Ethelwold, and that she approved and supported his actions wholeheartedly. For Ethelwold, the ultimate goal was not just introduction of the Benedictine Rule, but also the improvement of monastic standards and the extension of monasticism. A major aspect of his policy was the removal of the secular clerks from the existing monasteries, an area in which it is possible to view Elfrida as one of the major figures promoting reform.

The policy of removing the secular clerks from the monasteries was approved of by Edgar, who took the credit for it in many sources.[26] He considered himself a major reformer, musing on the state of the monasteries in a charter concerning Malmesbury Abbey, for example:

As I was lying awake studying the matter, my pious devotions were helped by the holy thought from above suddenly entering my mind that I should renew all the sacred monasteries in my kingdom. Not only are they visibly destroyed down to their wall tops with moss-cornered tiles and rotten roof beams, but also and more importantly, their insides had become almost completely neglected and emptied of worship of God. Indeed I have ejected the uneducated secular clergy who were not subject to the discipline of a religious life lived under a rule, and in very many places installed pastors of a more holy lineage, that is the brotherhood of monks. And in order that they might renew all these ruined temples, I have provided them with wealth in abundance from the revenues of the treasury.[27]

Edgar held the removal of the secular clergy as the primary requirement for the re-establishment of monasticism, and it is likely that Elfrida also held this view. It is almost unavoidable to escape the conclusion that it was the ascetic Ethelwold who instilled this idea into the mind of Edgar and, probably, also his queen.

Ethelwold identified the problem of the secular clerks early in his career, although he was not in a position to take any widespread action until appointed to his bishopric in 963. Not noted for his patience, he first attempted to persuade the clerks in his diocese to accept the Rule, perhaps not comprehending that others might not feel as strongly as he himself did. By 964, however, it was clear to him that the clerks were not simply prepared to abandon their comfortable lives for the existence of a monk and he decided to take more drastic action. According to Elfric's Life of St Ethelwold, the clerks in the Old Minster at Winchester were particularly offensive to the bishop. They refused to celebrate mass and took numerous wives, repudiating them when they tired of them.[28] The secular clerks spent their time feasting and enjoying themselves rather than performing their religious observations. Although this is likely to be an exaggeration of the behaviour of the clerks in order to show the bishop in a better light, their very presence rankled with Ethelwold and, in 964, he went to the king to ask permission for them to be removed.[29]

Edgar, raised on his tutor's antipathy to the clerks, proved sympathetic and sent one of his thegns, Wulfstan, to Winchester with Ethelwold to command the clerics either to leave or to become monks.[30] The pair arrived at the Old Minster with a deputation of monks from Abingdon and burst into the church, where the secular clerks were gathered, evidently forewarned. Ethelwold presented his ultimatum to the assembled clerks, with only three agreeing to stay and follow the Rule.[31] The bishop, unperturbed by this mass exodus, quickly set about installing his own monks at the Old Minster. Soon afterwards, he also expelled the secular clerks from the New Minster at Winchester and established nuns who followed the Rule at Nunnaminster.[32] There is a suggestion in the sources that Elfrida played a similar role in relation to the expulsion of the clerks at the New Minster as Edgar did with the Old Minster, with her signature as a witness to the New Minster's refoundation charter stating that she was 'with the king's approval establishing the monks in the same place, by the sending of my ambassador'.[33] Apparently the royal couple worked in concert, thereby playing a decisive role in the establishment of reform in Winchester, the premier city in England.

This was not to be the last that Ethelwold heard of the secular clerks, however, as those from the Old Minster appealed to Edgar to restore them to their homes.[34] These clerks had not reckoned on Ethelwold's close relationship with the king and, at a council at Winchester, St Dunstan held that the expulsion was correct. The clerks were next thwarted in their attempts to murder the bishop with poison, which, although he drank from the cup 'and immediately his face turned pale, and his bowels were greatly racked by the strength of the poison', he survived, becoming even more zealous in his approach after attributing his narrow escape to a miracle.[35] The fact that the expulsion remained very unpopular away from reformist circles is clear from the reaction taken against monasticism as soon as Edgar, Ethelwold's greatest patron and protector, was dead. Ethelwold was by no means the only churchman to come into conflict with the secular clerks, although his contemporary, Oswald, took a considerably less confrontational approach, seeking to persuade the clerks to follow the Rule through watching his example rather than by force.[36] He did, however, set out to found his own Benedictine houses, including Ramsey.[37] The re-establishment and foundation of new monasteries was another policy encouraged by both Edgar and Elfrida, who were often persuaded to give generously to the new houses.

Monasticism had been in great decline at the beginning of Edgar's reign but, by the time of his death, over forty monastic houses had reputedly been founded or re-established.[38] Even allowing for some exaggeration, this was a considerable achievement and one that could not have occurred without the support of the king and his wife. Ethelwold was a firm believer in the idea that any land that had once belonged to the Church always belonged to the Church and he quickly persuaded Edgar and Elfrida of the righteousness of this position. A good example of this policy can be seen in the example of Chertsey Abbey, which had been destroyed by the Vikings in the previous century, and the church had been burned.[39] According to William of Malmesbury,

> King Edgar, that nonpareil prince, who was not content with the new monasteries being built everywhere by himself or his bishops unless he also patched up the old ones, got it properly restored. He searched out from all corners the old documents which warranted him giving back to the monastery the estates which had been appropriated by certain nobles for their own use either through force or through the title of longstanding occupation.[40]

This policy helped restore land to the monasteries at little cost to the king or the Church and it must have seemed an excellent way of increasing the Church's prosperity. The monastery at Malmesbury, for example, had ten manors at Eastcott restored to it by Edgar, which had been leased out by the secular clerks at the Abbey.[41] Ethelwold was the main instigator of this policy, and used lawsuits and his knowledge of the king's favour to obtain what he wanted.[42] One of the monasteries that he personally re-established was Peterborough. According to the Anglo-Saxon Chronicle he, rather conveniently, found ancient writing referring to the original abbey stored in the walls of the ruined building, providing evidence of the monastery's earlier endowment.[43] Edgar also gave generously to the abbey.

Elfrida supported Ethelwold's policy wholeheartedly, interceding with Edgar on a number of occasions. The bishop, who was seemingly always trawling through old documents to find ancient Church privileges, on one occasion discovered that the freedom of Taunton had once been enjoyed by the see at Winchester.[44] This was a lucrative privilege and one that Ethelwold was anxious to recover, in spite of the fact that it had lapsed long ago. He went first to Edgar with his evidence of the ancient right but, on finding the king unmoved, turned to Elfrida for support. Given her closeness to the bishop, the queen went at once to the king to persuade him to allow the freedom to be renewed. Edgar was more amenable to his wife's pleas than those of his old tutor and agreed to do as the bishop asked. In the charter renewing the freedom of Taunton, it is recorded that

> then Bishop Aethelwold gave his royal lord 200 mancuses of gold and a silver cup worth five pounds in return for the renewal of this freedom, and to Aelfthryth [Elfrida], his wife, 50 mancuses of gold, in return for her help in his just mission.[45]

These were valuable presents and Elfrida's help was obviously appreciated. The queen also witnessed this charter, perhaps insisting on being present to witness Ethelwold's pleasure at the grant first hand. This incident would also have demonstrated to Elfrida how lucrative support of the Church could be and, as a political figure, her aid was probably never given entirely disinterestedly. She soon found a conflict of interests in relation to this particular grant, for which she was able to rely on Ethelwold's support and understanding.

Soon after the grant was made, she was approached by her kinswoman, Wulfgyth, who held land at Taunton with her husband, Leofric, which would be forfeited to the Church.[46] Moved by her kinswoman's concerns, Elfrida went to Ethelwold and persuaded him to let Wulfgyth and Leofric continue to hold their land at Taunton for life before it reverted to the Church. Ethelwold has a reputation for his uncompromising approach to land and privileges that he believed were ecclesiastical. The fact that he was prepared to drop a claim to land at the personal plea of Elfrida therefore demonstrates his respect and fondness for her.

Elfrida appears prominently in the documents of Edgar's reign that related to the Church reform and she was probably present at many of the councils and meetings at which the reform was discussed. Elfrida was certainly present at another council requested by Ethelwold, in which the privacy of the three monastic houses at Winchester was assured, in accordance with the Rule of St Benedict, by the demolition of several private houses in the city.[47] He was also able to persuade Edgar to allow for religious property to be re-adjusted among the religious houses in Winchester. According to a charter of King Edgar,

> here it is declared in this document how King Edgar caused the monasteries in Winchester to have their privacy secured for them by means of a space, after he had made them adopt the monastic life, by the grace of God, ordered it to be devised so that none of the monasteries involved should have any quarrel with any other, because of the spacing, but if the property of one monastery lay within the space assigned to another, then the superior of the monastery which took possession of the space should acquire the property of the other monastery by such exchange as might be agreeable to the community which owned the property.[48]

This policy would have appeared eminently reasonable to Ethelwold's orderly mind, and it is likely that Elfrida also saw the benefits of it and supported it. She was certainly present at the meeting in which it was agreed, and she witnessed Ethelwold granting two plots of land to the New Minster in exchange for its mill, which inconveniently lay in the space assigned to the Old Minster.[49] She also may have played a role in the negotiations between Abbot Ethelgar of the New Minster and Abbess Edith of Nunnaminster, where it was agreed that the abbot would give two mills to the abbess in return for diverting a watercourse from the nunnery to the New Minster. Elfrida certainly played a role in securing Edgar's consent for this transaction and, according to the charter, Abbot Ethelgar gave 'the king 120 mancuses of red gold in acknowledgement before the Lady Aelfthryth [Elfrida] and Bishop Aethelwold, in return for the land through which the water runs'.[50] Once again, this charter shows Elfrida working closely with Ethelwold in order to promote the religious reform in England.

Ethelwold and Elfrida were politically useful to each other during the religious reform and they seem to have shared similar views of the way in which the country should be run. This relationship developed through an interest in religious reform but quickly developed into a more lasting political alliance. Elfrida's politics during Edgar's reign are almost indistinguishable from those of Ethelwold and, until the end of her life, she protected his reputation and the policies that he stood for. He, in turn, sought to protect the queen politically and played a major role in the establishment of her queenship and her political position at her husband's court, something that ensured that she became the most politically prominent woman in tenth-century England.

1. The Anglo-Saxon kings from Edmund I to Edmund II Ironside, with kingship passing from father to son, brother to brother or uncle to nephew. Edmund Ironside, who was raised by his grandmother, Elfrida, was the last of his line until the accession of his half-brother, Edward the Confessor, in 1042. (Elizabeth Norton)

2. An Anglo-Saxon king enthroned. The kings of Wessex were initially wary of allowing a queen to sit beside them on the throne, preferring them to take a less prominent role. (Elizabeth Norton)

3. An Anglo-Saxon king presiding over his witan or council. Elfrida attended council meetings in the reigns of her husband and son. (Elizabeth Norton)

4. The coronation of King Edgar at Bath Abbey. Unusually for the Anglo-Saxon period, Elfrida, Edgar's queen, shared his coronation. (Elizabeth Norton)

5. King Alfred the Great. Ethelred II's famous ancestor proved singularly more successful in his approach to the Vikings. (Elizabeth Norton)

Right: 6. The Alfred Jewel, which is displayed in the Ashmolean Museum in Oxford, is one of the finest examples of Anglo-Saxon craftsmanship. (Elizabeth Norton)

Below: 7. A highly romanticised nineteenth-century depiction of the first meeting between Elfrida and Edgar, demonstrating the way in which their marriage continued to attract interest centuries after their deaths. (Elizabeth Norton)

VIRGI   NVM

8. Female saints from the Benedictional of St Ethelwold. This fine manuscript was commissioned by Bishop Ethelwold, Elfrida's friend and ally. This illustration provides a good idea of the dress of a tenth-century noblewoman. (Elizabeth Norton)

Above: 10. Elfrida's daughter-in-law, Emma of Normandy, and her second husband, Cnut. Emma, a particularly powerful queen, succeeded Elfrida in the role and may have modelled herself on her mother-in-law. (Elizabeth Norton)

Previous page: 9. King Edgar from a medieval manuscript. Elfrida's husband earned himself the nickname 'The Peaceable', thanks to a reign devoid of military conflict. (Elizabeth Norton)

11. Following his coronation in 973, Edgar moved his court to Chester in order to make a display of his imperial ambitions. He was rowed down the river by a number of kings and princes, over whom he claimed dominance. (Elizabeth Norton)

12. Corfe Castle. The later medieval castle was reputedly built on the site of Elfrida's house at Corfe, where her stepson was murdered. (Elizabeth Norton)

Previous page and this page: 13. and 14. Eighteenth- and nineteenth-century depictions of the murder of Edward the Martyr, both of which assign Elfrida a prominent place as the murderess. In reality, no contemporary sources actually assign her a role in the assassination. (Elizabeth Norton)

Next page: 15. Edward the Confessor was Elfrida's grandson and the last king of the royal house of Wessex. (John Brooks and Jonathan Reeve JR1117slide10001100)

7

IMPERIAL AMBITIONS

Elfrida's interests as queen were not purely religious. There is no doubt that she had political ambitions and Edgar encouraged her in this. The couple's attempts to found a legitimate royal family may, in part, be seen as a reflection of the imperial ambitions that Edgar increasingly began to display as his reign progressed.

In 966, when Elfrida had been married for around two years, much of the royal family and the court gathered at the New Minster at Winchester to celebrate its refoundation. The event would have been treated as a cause of celebration and Elfrida, who had by then borne Edgar a son, Edmund, attended with the infant. The witness list from this charter is particularly telling about Elfrida and her political aspirations: Edgar, of course, witnessed first, followed by Archbishop Dunstan.[1] Elfrida, as the fifth witness, would have been pleased to be accorded the position of highest-status woman, witnessing before the king's grandmother, Eadgifu, who had returned from retirement for the event. Something of considerably more interest is that the third witness was the infant Edmund, who witnessed as 'Edmund Aetheling, the legitimate son of the aforementioned king, flourishing in infantile age'. Edmund can only have been a few months old at the time, but the occasion was considered important enough for his young hand to be slowly moved over the parchment to make the sign of a cross in ink. After Elfrida's son came 'Edward Aetheling, begotten by the same king' and then 'Aelfthryth [Elfrida], the legitimate wife of the aforementioned king'. In these few simple lines, a very significant political point is made in the fact that the infant Edmund and his mother were stressed as 'legitimate' members of the royal family, while Edward, the son of Edgar's first wife, was not. Additionally, for Edmund to have witnessed before his elder half-brother when both were the sons of the king is telling of their respective statuses.

The New Minster Charter was drafted by Bishop Ethelwold, and it is possible that such stresses reflect his prejudices and his determination to promote Elfrida and her queenship. However, the charter was an important document and it is unlikely that Edgar would not have asked to see it or would not have been complicit in its composition. Even if he was ignorant of the contents, he can hardly have failed to grasp that his elder son was asked to witness after the baby Edmund, to whom he had already given the dynastically significant name of his famous father. When Elfrida's own son, Ethelred, later came to name his sons after his most revered predecessors as king, he named his second son Edmund after his grandfather, while the name Edward, after his great-grandfather, Edward the Elder, was used only for his second youngest son. This gives some evidence of the esteem in which the two former kings were respectively held in the tenth century, with Edmund being the more admired. Edgar was, of course, aware of this, and deliberately chose to prioritise his son by Elfrida over his son by Ethelflaed *Eneda*, the distinguishing feature between the two boys apparently being legitimacy.

This was not, in fact, an entirely new policy; Edward the Elder also selected the son of a more legitimate wife (Elfflaed) as his successor over the candidacy of his eldest son, Athelstan.[2] This may well have been due to consecration. Crowned in 964 or not, there can be no doubt that Edgar intended to prioritise his third wife and her offspring, something that attests to Elfrida's political dominance. The evidence of a genealogy of the West Saxon kings, composed during Edgar's reign, and which merely gives the names of Edgar's sons with no order of precedence except age, should not be taken as more authoritative than the important New Minster charter.[3]

Elfrida hoped that one of her sons would succeed Edgar in preference to the elder Edward. Motherhood was always an acceptable outlet for female power in the Anglo-Saxon period. Eadgifu had, of course, come to prominence under her sons, Edmund and Eadred. Elfrida's close relationship with Ethelwold was not her only political alliance and, following the birth of Edmund, she began to build a party around him at the expense of her stepson, Edward the Martyr. Although little evidence of these complex political alliances survives today, it is clear that both Elfrida and Ethelwold were actively cultivating support for her son. Elfrida gained particular support from the brothers Ealdormen, Elfhere and Elfheah.[4] Ealdorman Elfhere would remain a prominent ally of Elfrida's for several years and both must have been mutually useful to each other. Elfheah, who died during Edgar's reign, also made his support of Elfrida's position clear in his will, stating,

And to Aelfthryth the king's wife, his gefaedere, he grants the estate at Shirburn just as it stands; and to the elder Aetheling, the king's son and hers, thirty mancuses of gold and a sword; and to the younger the estate at Walkhampstead.[5]

The wording of the Will leaves the reader in no doubt that the only two Aethelings in England were Elfrida's two sons, Edmund and his younger brother Ethelred, who was born in around 968. The use of the word 'gefaedere' in relation to Elfrida is interesting since it denotes the relationship created between the parent and godparent of a child, or between two godparents. It seems not impossible that Elfheah's support was bought for Elfrida's party by making him godfather to her eldest son. Sadly, if this was so, the child did not live to get the benefit of this support, dying in 971 when he was aged around five. The death of Edmund, who was considered to be the king's heir by many, was a great blow to his parents both emotionally and politically, and it is telling that arrangements were made for him to be buried at Romsey, the religious house in which Elfrida had settled her stepdaughter, Ethelflaed, to whom she was close. The blow was doubly hard for Elfrida as, in the same year, her father also died, a man to whom she was close.

In spite of these losses, Elfrida continued to work politically to benefit her own family since, with a remaining son, she was able to transfer her ambitions to him. Another likely supporter of the candidacy of Elfrida's sons is Elfgifu, the former wife of King Eadwig. She left land in her Will, which was drawn up after 966, to the 'Aetheling', implying that there was then only one such child in England. Given Elfgifu's political affiliation to Bishop Ethelwold, she is unlikely to have been referring to Edward, instead either seeking to benefit Edmund before Ethelred's birth, or Ethelred after Edmund's death. Either way it was another vote of support for Elfrida and her children's legitimacy.

Edgar enjoyed a reputation for fierceness among his neighbours and this may account for part of the reason why he was never called upon to defend his country and why he soon earned the nickname 'the Peaceable'. According to a story by William of Malmesbury, Edgar was small in stature but very strong. One day, at a banquet, Kenneth, King of Scots, joked 'that it seemed extraordinary to him how so many provinces should be subject to such a sorry little fellow'.[6] News of this remark threw Edgar into a rage and he summoned Kenneth to his presence immediately, boiling with anger. Once Kenneth had arrived, Edgar offered to fight him with swords to demonstrate who was the stronger. The rage of the English king, who considered himself to be his overlord, was too much for Kenneth and he quickly fell on his knees, begging forgiveness. Edgar willingly forgave Kenneth, emerging the victor in a battle of wills rather than a contest of strength.

Regardless of the veracity of this story, the presence of Kenneth at Edgar's court is not impossible and can be considered to be part of the English king's ambition to present himself as an emperor of Britain. To modern eyes, used to viewing the island of Britain as divided into England, Wales and Scotland, this seems unlikely, but given that until only a few years before Edgar's birth, much of modern England had been divided into smaller kingdoms (with Mercia and Northumberland of course breaking away again under Eadwig), the idea that Wales and even Scotland could be incorporated into Edgar's kingdom in some form was not implausible in the mid-tenth century: Ecgbert, the founder of Edgar's dynasty, had managed to annex the lands of the 'West Welsh' in Cornwall to his own kingdom early in the ninth century.

According to William of Malmesbury, Edgar claimed dominance over more lands than any of his predecessors, although this dominance did not last long after his death.[7] He was able to build on the conquests of his predecessors, such as his grandfather, Edward the Elder, and uncle, King Athelstan, and to maintain the conditions for peace that they had established.[8] It is a sign of his competence that his reign is recorded as almost empty of incident, and it is his coronation in 973 that is remembered as the first great secular event of the reign.[9]

Anglo-Saxon kings were generally crowned soon after their accession in order to secure their hold on the throne. These ceremonies were probably hurried affairs with only minimal organisation, and Edgar himself would have also gone through one of these ceremonies in 959. Normally, this would be the last coronation of the reign but Edgar, influenced by the ideas of the religious reform and his imperial ambitions, resolved to be crowned again in 973 after he had been king for nearly fourteen years. This coronation was the biggest event of the reign and would have served, as the earlier New Minster charter celebration did, to highlight the magnificence of the royal family and Edgar's dynasty. The coronation was a celebration of Edgar's dominance of England and other areas of Britain, but it was also a demonstration of his personal majesty and his wife, Elfrida, was expected to play a prominent role.

For his coronation, Edgar chose the Roman city of Bath, playing on its Imperial past to reflect his own aspirations. This ruined city had always excited the imagination of the English, and it is generally assumed that the early Anglo-Saxon poem *The Ruin* refers to it. This poem shows clearly the awe that was felt for the ancient city, referring to it, poetically, as the work of giants and which, even in its ruinous state, had seen kingdoms rise and fall.[10] It was the perfect location for what was to be the most important ceremonial event of the reign. As well as wanting to present himself as an Emperor, Edgar also wanted to highlight his similarity, as an earthly king, to Christ. The choice of 973 for the coronation year was deliberately chosen as the year in which Edgar turned thirty. In the tenth century, Christ was generally held to have been crucified in his thirtieth year, and the similarity of Edgar's age highlighted his role as a Christ-like figure on earth. The approaching millennium was also a factor in the decision behind the coronation, again ensuring that the occasion was considered particularly auspicious.

There were also other Biblical references attached to the coronation and these had a direct bearing on Elfrida's own role as Edgar's queen. The coronation service was probably revised by Bishop Ethelwold and, because of this, the coronation of the queen features prominently in the rite.[11] Ethelwold's revised coronation *ordo* stressed the importance of the queen's role as a helper to the king and, for the first time in Anglo-Saxon history, raised the importance of the king's wife to near equality with the king.[12] Elfrida and Ethelwold may have had to work hard to ensure that Edgar saw the wisdom of including such a prominent role for his wife in the coronation ceremony. Reaction to the coronation of Judith of Francia as Queen of Wessex had nearly cost Edgar's great-great-grandfather his throne, although by the mid-tenth century it was not unheard of for a powerful queen to undergo some ceremony of consecration, as the probable examples of Elfflaed, Ethelflaed of Damerham and even Elfrida herself on her marriage show. There was also a very recent imperial precedent since, on 14 April 972, the Byzantine princess Theophano was crowned as Holy Roman Empress in Rome following her marriage to the Emperor Otto II.[13] This would have been a great spectacle and one for which Edgar might, even under normal circumstances, have received reports. Perhaps significantly, St Oswald was present in Rome during 972 on a visit to receive his pallium as Archbishop of York. He may well have witnessed the coronation or, at least, have heard first-hand reports of it, and probably returned to England filled with news of imperial splendour. Edgar, already interested in appearing as an emperor, was very interested in this example of how an emperor should act and it swung his opinion towards the coronation of Elfrida.

Like Edgar, Elfrida appears to have undergone an earlier ceremony of consecration, which would have been focussed on her fertility and designed to enhance the throne worthiness of her offspring. The 973 coronation was, however, an innovation, focussing as it did on the majesty of the royal couple and elevating the royal wife above her previous primary role of royal mother. In 973 Elfrida also became the very first woman to be crowned, with certainty, as Queen of England, and accounts of the coronation demonstrate that it was glorious.

The coronation occurred on 11 May 973, attended by the bishops, abbots, abbesses and much of the nobility.[14] Edgar was led into the church by abbots dressed in 'snow-white albs covered with purple', with the abbesses and their nuns, and then priests following behind. Once inside the church, two bishops took Edgar's hands and led him forward while the company sang out in praise. On reaching the altar Edgar prostrated himself on the floor as Dunstan, stepping forward sang a *Te Deum*. The archbishop was weeping as he carried out his task 'because he realised that this people did not deserve to have a ruler so humble and so wise'. Once the *Te Deum* was finished, Edgar was lifted to his feet by the bishops and, in response to Dunstan's questions, made three vows, stating that

> I promise in the first instance that the church of God and the entire Christian populace shall under my authority keep true peace at all times; I also promise that I shall proscribe theft and all manner of wickedness for persons of all stations; and thirdly, that in all judgements I shall enjoin justice and mercy, so that our kind and merciful God shall grant his mercy to me and you.

The bishops prayed before the king was crowned and anointed, as well as being given a ring and sword by Dunstan and then a sceptre and a rod. The company then heard mass, celebrated by Dunstan himself before the company removed themselves to the coronation banquet.

The account of the coronation in the Life of St Oswald does not, in fact, mention the coronation of the queen, although, given its prominence in the *Ordo* used, it is certain that time was found to also consecrate Elfrida. She was greatly in evidence at the coronation banquet. Edgar, the centre of attention, sat in splendour with the bishops, ealdormen and other noblemen, while Elfrida, in another chamber, sat with the abbots and abbesses. She was lavishly attired for the occasion, 'being dressed in linen garments and robed splendidly, adorned with a variety of precious stones and pearls, she loftily surpassed the other ladies present', with a 'regal bearing'. Given that Edgar had commanded that all the higher ranks of the nobility and the Church in his kingdom attend the coronation, Elfrida had additional cause for triumph since her rival, Wulfthryth, and the former queen's kinswoman, Wulfhild, would have sat at her table – in places inferior to the queen – among the abbesses. For Elfrida, her consecration in 973 and, perhaps, the precedence that she was granted so obviously over the king's former wife once again demonstrated to everyone that it was she who was 'the legitimate wife of the king'.

The coronation celebrations were not the only grand ceremonial event of 973 and, soon afterwards, Edgar joined his navy and sailed for another ceremony that was scheduled at Chester.[15] Although she is not recorded in the sources, Elfrida may well have insisted upon joining Edgar for the further festivities. According to the twelfth-century chronicle of Florence of Worcester, Edgar

sailed around the north part of Britain with a large fleet, and landed at Chester. Eight petty kings, namely, Kynath, King of Scots, Malcolm, King of the Cumbrians, Maccus, King of several isles, and five others named Dufnall, Siferth, Huwall, Jacob and Juchill, met him there as he had appointed, and swore that they would be faithful to him, and assist him by land and by sea. On a certain day they attended him into a boat, and when he had placed them at the oars, he himself took the helm and skilfully steered it down the River Dee, and thus, followed by the whole company of earls and nobles, in this order went from the palace to the monastery of St John the Baptist. After having prayed there, he returned with the same pomp to the palace. As he was entering it, he is reported to have said to his nobles, that then his successors might boast themselves to be kings of the English, when, attended by so many kings, they should enjoy the pomp of such honours.[16]

This is the most famous event of Edgar's reign, and the image of the king steering a boat rowed by eight other kings is a powerful one. The ceremony included oaths, binding the other kings to Edgar and effectively making him their overlord.[17] Edgar insisted upon this display of his power to make a point both at home and abroad that he was the imperial ruler of Britain and, according to William of Malmesbury, it was a demonstration that made him famous both in England and on the Continent.[18]

Edgar's meeting of the British kings at Chester presents a powerful image, but it was not the only demonstration of his imperial ambitions, and several of the sources from his reign emphasise an imperial unity across England. Soon after his coronation and the Chester meeting, Edgar further demonstrated his power by introducing a widespread reform of the coinage and issuing a new lawcode, known as IV Edgar.[19] The IV Edgar lawcode is unique in the idea of unity across Britain that it presents. For example, clause 2.2 states that 'this measure is to be common to all the nation, whether Englishmen, Danes or Britons, in every province of my dominion'.[20] Clause 14.2 follows up this theme with a claim that 'this addition is to be common to all of us who inhabit these islands'.[21] This was the first time that an Anglo-Saxon king had presumed to legislate for anyone other than the English and shows Edgar's ambition for power. Certainly, he was the first king who could truly call himself King of England, although some of his other claims to overlordship across Britain are doubtful. By the same token, Elfrida is the first woman who can truly be considered to have been Queen of England.

Edgar was still a young man at the time of his coronation and both he and Elfrida expected him to live for several more years, at least until their son, Ethelred, reached maturity. It must have come as a shock to everyone, therefore, when the king 'was suddenly snatched from this world, having with him a few thegns and companions' on 8 July 975.[22] The cause of Edgar's sudden death is not recorded although, given the high number of Anglo-Saxon kings who died young, there may have been a hereditary weakness. Whatever the cause, it was a disaster, with the near-contemporary Life of St Oswald lamenting that 'the commonwealth of the entire realm was shaken'.

No one can have been as shaken as the queen. If he was not already in her custody, she would have immediately taken steps to secure the possession of her seven-year-old son, Ethelred, whom she and her followers viewed as Edgar's heir. This was not how everyone saw matters, however, and Elfrida was all too aware that she faced an uphill struggle to secure the throne for her child.

8

THE HEIRS OF KING EDGAR

The death of Edgar, when he was still only in his early thirties, threw the country into confusion, as well as leaving the succession to the throne wide open.

With the exception of his two young sons, Edgar had no close male kin and certainly none who could conclusively establish themselves as King of England. There were no fixed rules of succession in Anglo-Saxon England other than the fact that the king should be an 'Aetheling', which was the son of a king. The evidence of both the ninth and tenth centuries shows that, additionally, an adult king was preferred to a minor. Edgar himself, along with his brother Eadwig, had been overlooked due to their age on the death of their father, King Edmund, and Edmund was instead succeeded by his adult brother Eadred. Edgar's own great-grandfather, Alfred the Great, had benefited from this preference for adult kings and had succeeded his elder brother, Ethelred I, ahead of his predecessor's infant sons. In 975, however, the only adult members of the royal family were the surviving descendants of Ethelred I, and a reversion from the line of Alfred was never likely to have been a popular solution. In reality, Edgar's only possible successors were Edward and Ethelred. Edward cannot have been more than around fourteen or fifteen years old and Ethelred was probably seven. It would have been clear to everyone that some sort of regency would be required with the accession of either boy, something unprecedented among the recent history of the kings of Wessex.

As the sons of different mothers, the two boys were also on alternative sides in the political factions that had developed in Edgar's reign.[1] Elfrida, naturally, supported the claims of her own child, Ethelred, and she was joined in this support by Bishop Ethelwold and her kinsman, Ealdorman Elfhere, among others. Interestingly, Dunstan and the family of Elfrida's first husband, Ealdorman Ethelwold, aligned themselves with Edward, suggesting that through her rivalry with the archbishop the queen had become estranged from her first husband's family and her own elder children, which would account for the later absence of her elder sons from their half-brother's court.

Dunstan and Edward's other supporters argued that, as the elder son, Edward was the more suited to kingship and also that his age meant he would be able to take up the reins of kingship more quickly that his younger half-brother. Edward's age was a major advantage for his candidacy and Elfrida and her supporters therefore resorted to being rather more creative in their attacks on the elder prince's claims. They were almost certainly the source of stories denigrating his mother to the status of a concubine, a very common means of attack on a rival's claims in the Anglo-Saxon period.[2] That this argument had already been formulated during Edgar's reign is clear from the attempts to prioritise Elfrida and her children as Edgar's legitimate family, and this would have been immediately stressed after Edgar's death in order to imply that Edward was less throne-worthy. There was certainly a recent precedent to this when Edward the Elder was succeeded by Elfweard, his eldest son by his second wife, a man who survived his father by only sixteen days.[3] Edward's eldest son, Athelstan, was only able to press his claim after his half-brother's death, and then only through the aid of powerful Mercian noblemen.[4] According to William of Malmesbury, 'The ground of this opposition, as they affirm, was that Athelstan was born of a concubine.'[5]

Attacks were levelled against Athelstan, claiming that his mother, Ecgwyna, had not been Edward the Elder's wife and was, instead, merely his concubine. Ecgwyna does not always seem to have been regarded as a concubine and William of Malmesbury had heard that she was an 'illustrious lady', and thus apparently a noblewoman[6]. Alfred the Great regarded his young grandson as legitimate when he was born, taking an interest in his upbringing and knighting him while still in his early childhood.[7] None of these facts suggest that Athelstan was always considered illegitimate, and an idea of his illegitimacy appears to have only grown up with the repudiation of his mother following his father's accession, and the emphasis laid on the second wife's status as a legitimate wife. Elfrida would have had knowledge of this recent history and recognised the parallels. Her stepson's mother, Ethelflaed *Eneda*, who appears to have been a noblewoman like Ecgwyna, was also denigrated and it may be that the origins of stories claiming that Edward was the son of a ravished nun began in 975. Such a denigration certainly happened in the early eleventh century following the death of Cnut in 1035, who left sons by two still living wives. The second wife, Emma of Normandy, claimed that the first wife had been merely a concubine and that her son, Harold, was, in fact the son of a servant rather than the king.[8]

Edward's 'illegitimacy' may not have been the only reason for people supporting Ethelred's candidacy for the throne. According to the Life of St Oswald, which is generally favourable to him, it was recorded that

> certain of the chief men of this land wished to elect as king the king's elder son, Edward by name; some of the nobles wanted the younger, because he appeared to all gentler in speech and deeds. The elder, in fact, inspired in all not only fear but even terror, for [he scourged them] not only with words but truly with dire blows, and especially his own men dwelling with him.[9]

This does not present a very favourable picture of the teenage Edward and he was known for the violence he inflicted on others, especially his own supporters in his household. The Life of St Oswald dates from the early eleventh century and so is a much more contemporary source than later accounts of Edward's personality, such as the twelfth-century Eadmer, who claimed that Edward was like his father in character.[10]

Elfrida, Bishop Ethelwold and Ealdorman Elfhere actively campaigned for Ethelred's accession following Edgar's death. Given Ethelred's extreme youth, they must have quickly become aware that they were fighting a losing battle and some sort of compromise was reached early on with Edward's supporters. Edward was crowned in around March 976, nearly a year after his father's death, while Ethelred was, at the same time, given the lands that traditionally belonged to the king's sons.[11] This may have been a recognition of Ethelred as Edward's heir and, in 976, was probably the best that Elfrida and her supporters could hope for. She was certainly not content, however, with William of

Malmesbury recording that Edward was elevated by Dunstan 'in opposition, as it is said, to the will of some of the nobility and of his stepmother'.[12]

Dunstan and his supporters hoped that Edward's coronation would neutralise support for Ethelred and bring the country back into order. This did not prove to be the case, however, and the country quickly slipped into a state of near civil war. Elfrida's whereabouts during this period are unknown and she may have retreated from the court with Ethelred, perhaps moving to her house at Corfe, where she and the boy were living two years later. Corfe was well within her family's sphere of influence in the West Country and she would have been able to meet, on occasion, with her brother, who also left court at the same time, apparently occupying himself with the continuing work in relation to his foundation of Tavistock Abbey.

Bishop Ethelwold's reaction is unknown, although he still features in charters from the reign and may have accepted the *status quo*.[13] He remained close to Elfrida, and it is likely that both the bishop and the queen continued to hope for Ethelred's future elevation. Certainly, in the only account of Elfrida's whereabouts during Edward's brief reign, she appears with Ethelwold, who brought both her and the young Ethelred to Ely with him on a visit to the monastery.[14] This visit seems not dissimilar to Ethelwold's attempts to show the young Edgar, his pupil, the ruinous state into which monasticism had fallen and the suspicion must be that the bishop was tutoring Ethelred in the same way as he had done his father. Both Ethelwold and Elfrida appear to have taken an active role in the young prince's education and they must have hoped that he would one day show himself to be as favourable and useful to religious reform as his father had been.

It was Ealdorman Elfhere who truly kept Ethelred's claim alive, and he, caught off guard by Edward's coronation, exploded into violence against the new king's regime and the interests of his supporters.[15] Elfhere, who was related to Elfrida, was a particularly powerful nobleman, as can be seen from the fact that a number of charters and other documents relating to Mercia during the reign of King Edgar, where Elfhere held his ealdordom, refer to the requirement that he gave his consent to the transaction.[16] According to the Anglo-Saxon Chronicle's account of Edward's reign,

> in his days, because of his youth, God's adversaries, Ealdorman Aelfhere and many others broke God's laws, and impeded monastic rule, and dissolved monasteries, and drove away monks, and put to flight God's servants, whom earlier King Edgar ordered the holy bishop Aethelwold to establish. And over and again widows were robbed, and many wrongs and injustices arose up thereafter, and after that it always got much worse.[17]

Elfhere's attacks on the monasteries and the reform as a whole cannot have been a policy that either Elfrida or Bishop Ethelwold could condone, and this may account for their absence from the sources regarding this movement. In a twentieth-century study of his actions, it was also pointed out that Elfhere's own religious affiliations might not have been so clear cut and that, instead, his actions were governed by the fact that he found himself on the opposing side in the succession dispute to the leading churchmen and that 'his reaction was to attack the Mercian monasteries; not because he was an enemy of monasticism as such, but because there he could hurt his political opponents where they were most vulnerable'.[18] In this analysis, Elfhere's actions should not be considered to be an 'anti-monastic reaction'; instead, he was probably also carrying out a deliberate policy designed to increase support for Ethelred, something that both Elfrida and Ethelwold could tentatively support. Edgar's death opened the way for the anti-monastic feeling that had developed to become manifest.[19] There was a great deal of resentment by many noblemen towards the new wealth and power of the reformed monastic houses, and Elfhere exploited this, perhaps hoping to build a rebellion strong enough to place Ethelred on the throne instead of his half-brother, Edward. Certainly, his attacks won popular support, suggesting that the re-establishment of monasticism had been far from universally popular.[20]

There was a very recent precedent for the replacement of one brother with another, and Dunstan must have been uncomfortably aware of his own role in Edgar's rebellion against his brother Eadwig. Edgar's rebellion in 957 had served to place him on the throne of Mercia, dividing Eadwig's kingdom in half. This was also not the only precedent for a rebellion by a kinsman against the reigning king, and both Edward and Ethelred's supporters would have been aware of the examples from recent history. Elfhere's actions must have looked, somewhat uncomfortably to Dunstan and his supporters, like the actions of Ethelwold, son of King Ethelred I, in 899.

According to the Anglo-Saxon Chronicle, following the death of Alfred the Great, his eldest son, Edward the Elder, succeeded to the throne:

then Aethelwold, his [Edward the Elder's] father's brother's son, rode and seized the manor at Wimborne and at Twinham without leave of the king and his councillors. Then the king rode with an army until he camped at Badbury, near Wimborne, and Aethelwold stayed inside that manor with the men who had given him their allegiance, and had barricaded all the gates against him, and said that he would either live there or die there. Then under cover of that he stole away by night and sought out the raiding army [Vikings] in Northumbria. And the king ordered him to be ridden after, and he could not be overtaken then.[21]

Ethelwold attempted to win the crown for himself by stirring up trouble across the country. His continuing rebellion was a major threat to the early years of Edward the Elder's kingship and was only resolved when, in 903, Ethelwold and the Danish king of East Anglia were killed in battle.[22] Another similar succession dispute occurred when Edwin, the full brother of Edward the Elder's second son and chosen successor, Elfweard, attempted to snatch the crown from King Athelstan: a bid for the crown that ended in the younger prince's murder.

It has been suggested that political murders were much more common than usually claimed in succession disputes and, certainly, two such disputes in the eleventh century ended in the suspiciously sudden deaths of the participants. In 1016, for example, the Danish invader, Cnut, and Elfrida's grandson, Edmund II, vied for the throne until an agreement was made to split the country between them. Within a few weeks Edmund was dead and Cnut king of the whole of England. Although not all reports ascribe Edmund's death to murder, it was certainly a convenient death for Cnut and one that should not be taken entirely at face value.[23] Another grandson of Elfrida's, Alfred, was murdered when he attempted to claim the throne from Harold I in 1036.[24] Rebellion and murder were therefore used throughout the Anglo-Saxon period to resolve succession disputes, and it is possible that Elfhere's actions were a deliberate attempt to de-stabilise Edward's government and place Ethelred on the throne in his stead.

Elfhere's rebellion was primarily aimed at the newly reformed monasteries and, according to the Life of St Oswald, he forcibly ejected the monks and allowed the secular clerks to return.[25] He was not the only nobleman involved in the attacks on the monasteries and there appears to have been a great deal of ill feeling among the nobility towards the reformed houses.[26] Despite the attention given to the attacks and the alarm they caused, Elfhere was only strong enough to attack those houses within his own ealdordom of Mercia.[27] He was resisted in eastern Mercia by Elfrida's former brother-in-law, Ealdorman Ethelwine, and his brother Elfwold.[28] According to the Life of St Oswald, matters advanced so far that Ethelwine raised an army, with himself at its head, while Elfwold went to Winchester to attempt to enlist the support of Bishop Ethelwold, suggesting that Elfhere's actions served only to divide Ethelred's supporters. He was unable to achieve the accession of Ethelred, with his actions instead contributing to the general feeling of misery and chaos that surrounded Edward's reign.

According to a number of sources, a comet was seen soon after Edward's succession, which was held to bode ill for the country.[29] Soon afterwards, crops failed, leading to famine.[30] These events were taken as evil omens. Dunstan was also troubled by the return of the secular clerks who, following Edgar's death, appealed against their expulsion from the monasteries.[31] The clerks had, apparently, badly misjudged Dunstan's own commitment to the reform and believed that they might be able to overturn Edgar's reforms in the new reign. The archbishop, hoping to rid himself of the problem of the clerks, called a synod at Winchester, which decided against them.[32]

A second council was called at Calne in 978 to decide the matter once and for all. This proved to be calamitous and, as the various parties debated angrily in an upper chamber of a house, 'the floor with its beams and supporters gave way suddenly and fell to the ground. All fell with it except Dunstan, who alone escaped unhurt by standing on a single rafter, which retained its position. The rest were either killed or maimed for life.'[33] The accident at Calne may have settled the question of the secular clerks once and for all with the deaths of their leaders but, in all other respects, it was a disaster for King Edward. Edward's former tutor, Bishop Sidemann of Crediton had already died the previous year and the disaster at Calne further thinned the ranks of his supporters.[34] Most of Edward's council were present at Calne, and were either killed or terribly injured.

It was the accident at Calne, above all other events of the reign, that allowed the young king's opponents to once again look towards his half-brother, Ethelred, who was living with Elfrida at Corfe.

9

THE MURDER OF EDWARD
THE MARTYR

Elfrida was at Corfe when word reached her of the Calne floor
accident in early 978. Corfe, in Dorset, was well within the area
of her family's political interests, something which was desirable
given the turmoil following Edgar's death. The steep hillside on
which her house reportedly stood also allowed both for defence
and excellent visibility of the surrounding area. It was there that
what was arguably the most traumatic political event of the late
tenth century was to be played out.

In spite of their obvious political opposition, the relationship
between Edward and Elfrida had not entirely broken down by
978, something that does indeed suggest that they had come to an
agreement whereby the young king acknowledged his half-brother
as his heir. Certainly, relations were cordial enough to ensure that,
on 18 March 978, Edward, who was then aged around seventeen
or eighteen, set out with a small escort to visit his stepmother.
A number of accounts describe that visit, each with increasingly
elaborate detail, and from them it is necessary to piece together
the facts behind Edward's visit to Elfrida at Corfe, and all that
happened there.

The Anglo-Saxon Chronicle contains the earliest reference to Edward's murder. The entry for 978 in Manuscript A of the Chronicle dates to at least before *c.* 1001–1013, and may, in fact, be even more contemporary.[1] It is certainly the earliest surviving edition of the Chronicle and therefore a useful starting point in any study of the murder. According to Manuscript A, 'Here King Edward was killed in this same year his brother, the atheling Aethelred, succeeded to the kingdom.'[2] Manuscript A is echoed in its sparse account by Manuscript C, which gives similarly little information except for stating that the king was 'martyred' rather than merely 'killed'.[3] Neither of these accounts are particularly helpful, save for highlighting that Edward was popularly known to have been murdered throughout England soon after the actual event occurred. These two accounts go no way to blaming Elfrida for the crime or, in fact, anyone.

It is therefore necessary to look in manuscript E of the Chronicle for a fuller account. According to this, 'King Edward was killed in the evening-time on 18 March at Corfe "passage", and they buried him at Wareham without any royal honours.'[4] This account, although again brief, establishes the fact that the murder took place in the evening and, ominously, that it occurred at Corfe. It would have been well known that Elfrida lived at Corfe and this reference is therefore telling. If this entry could be proved to be contemporary it would show that Elfrida was associated with the murder almost immediately after it took place. Manuscript E, however, was produced some time after 1116 and was based on a lost earlier copy.[5] It is therefore unclear when this entry was actually composed, and impossible now for it to be securely dated. Since the other, certainly early, editions of the Chronicle give such a brief account of the murder it seems likely that the reference to

Corfe, and thus Elfrida's involvement, was a later addition. This is certainly not implausible, and embellishments were common in later editions of medieval manuscripts: the earliest version of the *History of the Church of Abingdon*, for example, merely claims that Edward 'was undeservedly killed by the treachery of wicked men', while a later version, dating to the thirteenth century, had been elaborated to declare that he was 'translated to Heaven through martyrdom by the trickery of his step-mother Aelfthryth'.[6]

The Anglo-Saxon Chronicle is not the only early source to give details concerning the murder of Edward the Martyr, and the earliest full account appears in the Life of St Oswald by Byrhtferth of Ramsey. This account was produced in the early eleventh century while Ethelred was still on the throne and has been described as based on eyewitness evidence.[7] It is therefore worth quoting Byrhtferth's account in full:

Meanwhile nine and five month had run out and the tenth moon was shining for mortals after he [Edward] had been elected; the zealous thegns of his brother rose up against him when he was hastening to come to talk with his beloved brother. Treacherous and evil, they sought the life of the innocent youth, whom Christ predestined and fore-ordained to share a martyr's dignity. When a certain day was nearing evening; the illustrious and elected king came as we have said to the house where his much loved brother dwelt with the queen, desiring the consolation of brotherly love; there came out to meet him, as was fitting, nobles and chief men, who stayed with the queen, his mother. They formed among them a wicked plan, for they possessed minds so accursed and such diabolical blindness that they did not fear to lay hands on the lord's anointed. Armed men surrounded him on all sides, and with them also stood the cupbearer to perform his humble office. The revered king indeed had with him very few thegns, for he feared no one, trusting 'in the lord and the might of his power'.

He was versed in divine law, by the teaching of Bishop Sidemann, and he was also strong and vigorous in body. And when his betrayers encircled him, just as the Jews once surrounded the supreme Christ, he sat undaunted on his horse. Certainly a single frenzy was in them, and a like insanity. Then the worst of villanies and the fierce madness of the devilish enemy was inflamed in the hearts of the venomous thegns; then the poisoned arrows of the crime of Pilates rose up very cruelly against the lord and against his anointed, who had been elected to defend the kingdom and empire of this most sweet race on his father's death. The thegns then holding him, one drew him on the right towards him as if he wished to give him a kiss, but another seized roughly his left hand and also wounded him. And he shouted, so far as he could: 'What are you doing – breaking my right arm?' And suddenly leapt from his horse and died.[8]

Byrhtferth gives the most detailed account of the way in which Edward died, and this has come to be the accepted version of events. It is also, according to a detailed analysis of remains believed to be Edward's, an accurate account.

In 1931 human bones were unearthed during excavations at Shaftesbury Abbey, which proved to have belonged to a man between 5 feet 6 and 5 feet 8 inches tall and aged around seventeen (and certainly no more than twenty-one).[9] These were then examined as though part of a criminal investigation and the injuries found were linked to the account in the Life of St Oswald. Edward's bones were found to have multiple injuries.

His left arm was broken, supposedly where it had been seized by one of his assailants, and his thigh fractured from being forced down into his saddle.[10] According to the examination, the body then rolled forward over the saddle and the left foot became trapped in the stirrup. The unconscious or dead Edward was dragged along the ground as his horse bolted causing further fractures to his leg. The examination of the bones suggests that the young king suffered a particularly unpleasant death.

The account in the Life of St Oswald therefore provides an early account of the king's death that appears, on the whole, believable. From an examination of the text and the bones themselves a sequence of events has been produced.[11] First, a man on Edward's left seized his left hand violently before stabbing him, breaking his arm in the process. A second man standing on the king's right then made a move as if kissing the king, unbalancing him in the saddle as he did so. The group of assassins drew in closely around the king to shield him from the view of onlookers and it was then that Edward cried out that his right arm was also being broken. Edward's horse, which was panicked by the noise and violence, broke free, and he was seen by onlookers to fall from his horse, his left foot becoming trapped as he did so, causing him to be dragged along the ground for some distance.

The Life of St Oswald places the murder firmly at Elfrida's house and claims that it was carried out by 'noble and chief men, who stayed with the queen'.[12] What is does not do is actually state that she carried out the murder herself. When the Life of St Oswald was written, Ethelred was still alive and it would have been impossible to fully implicate the mother of the reigning king. However, equally, the Life is far from positive towards Ethelred and could have given a greater role to Elfrida if, indeed, she had had one:

it is telling that, throughout, the author of the Life refers to the murderers as men rather than women, for example in the claim that 'those madmen who had done the deed' were later punished by God.[13] In contrast, by the end of the eleventh century, Elfrida's involvement was commonly accepted.[14] Given some of the lurid stories that became attached to the queen's name, it is debateable how far this evidence should be believed.

The first account to actually name Elfrida as the instigator of the crime is the mid-eleventh-century Life of St Dunstan by Osbern. According to Osbern, Edward was 'killed by a stepmother's deceit'.[15] This is merely a brief mention of Elfrida's supposed guilt, but said in such a way that it implies that her guilt was, by then, common knowledge.[16] Clearly, therefore, following Ethelred's death in 1016, accounts of the murder became more open about Elfrida's alleged involvement, moving on from merely placing her at the scene to naming her as the main instigator. This was a common trend in the mid- to late eleventh century, and Adam of Bremen, writing between 1072 and 1081, claimed that she was involved, although blaming Ethelred himself for the actual murder.[17] It seems improbable that the ten-year-old Ethelred was actually the main conspirator in the death of his brother, although it was likely carried out for his benefit. The earliest elaborate account of Elfrida's role occurs in the late eleventh-century *Passion of Edward the Martyr*, which claims that she planned the murder, leaving her followers to carry out the crime.[18] In all the late eleventh-century accounts, Elfrida was held out as the leading plotter behind the murder, and every post-Conquest account was also certain of her guilt.[19]

Some post-Conquest accounts give little detail of the murder, save that it was planned by the queen herself. Simeon of Durham, for example, claimed that Edward was killed on her command.[20] The early twelfth-century writer, Eadmer, also claimed that he was killed at Elfrida's behest, as did Florence of Worcester.[21] These accounts make it clear that Elfrida's 'guilt' was common knowledge, but some later accounts do give further details of the murder not previously provided. The early twelfth-century historian, William of Malmesbury, for example, added the following details:

> The woman, however, with a stepmother's hatred, began to mediate a subtle stratagem, in order that not even the title of king might be wanting to her child, and to lay a treacherous snare for her son-in-law, which she accomplished in the following manner. He was returning home, tired with the chase, and gasping with thirst from the exercise, while his companions were following the dogs in different directions as it happened, when hearing that they dwelt in a neighbouring mansion, the youth proceeded thither at full speed, unattended and unsuspecting, as he judged of others by his own feelings. On his arrival, alluring him to her with female blandishments, she made him fix his attention upon herself, and after saluting him while he was eagerly drinking from the cup which had been presented, the dagger of an attendant pierced him through. Dreadfully wounded, with all his remaining strength he spurred his horse in order to join his companions; when one foot slipping he was dragged by the other through the winding paths, while the steaming blood gave evidence of his death to his followers.[22]

William of Malmesbury, along with a number of post-Conquest accounts, actually places Elfrida at the scene of the crime and helping in the murder in some way. Henry of Huntingdon also believed that she was involved in the actual murder, stating, 'It is reported that his stepmother, that is the mother of King Aethelred, stabbed him with a dagger while she was in the act of offering him a cup to drink.'[23] This account actually has Elfrida as the murderess, stabbing the king with her own hand.

Despite the increasing elaboration of Elfrida's guilt, the post-Conquest accounts of the murder still retain similarities with the account in the Life of St Oswald. The murder always occurs at the place where Elfrida lives when Edward is visiting his half-brother with only a small number of attendants. In all accounts, the deed is carried out as he arrived, before he even has time to dismount, and Edward is always stabbed. Even the latest, most detailed, account of the murder retains these key elements. This account is contained in Gaimar's *History of the English*.

According to Gaimar, Edward was dining in Wiltshire with a dwarf called Wolstanet.[24] During the dinner, the dwarf refused to play for Edward and the king grew so angry with him that he fled. Wolstanet took a horse from the house where Edward was dining and rode to Elfrida's house, which was nearby.[25] Edward, who was still fuming at the dwarf's insolence, set out in pursuit and, arriving at his stepmother's residence, asked for him. According to Gaimar, Edward found few people at the house but the queen came out to greet him and asked him to dismount and enter her house while she sent her own people to search for the renegade.[26] Edward, suspicious of his stepmother's motives, refused to dismount, preferring to stay in the courtyard on his horse.[27] Undaunted, the queen insisted on providing him with a drink and he agreed, providing that she drank from the cup first to prove that it was not poisoned.[28] Elfrida, perhaps feigning hurt at her stepson's mistrust, had her servant fill a drinking horn and drank from it before passing it to Edward. Edward drank deeply but, as he leant forward to pass the horn back to his hostess, an assailant stabbed him.[29] The young king cried out in surprise and pain, and his horse bolted, carrying him off on the road towards Cirencester.[30]

Gaimar's account of Edward's murder is by far the most detailed and is the only story to refer to the dwarf.[31] This account places Elfrida among those surrounding Edward's horse and, once again, attributes the blame to her. It seems likely that the story of the dwarf was an invention by Gaimar. However, other elements of the story do agree with the majority of the other accounts, and it was almost certainly based on earlier sources.

All of the accounts of the murder of Edward the Martyr from the mid-eleventh century place the blame for the planning of the murder on Elfrida herself. In these accounts, she is portrayed as the archetypal wicked stepmother, ambitious for her own child at the expense of her stepson. However, earlier accounts are not so explicit. It seems safe to assume that the murder occurred at Corfe, since this was included in accounts contemporary to Ethelred. Equally, it appears that Edward went there specifically to see his brother and that he was, at the very least, attacked by some of the thegns who supported his half-brother. This does not, however, mean that Elfrida was aware of the plans in advance, or even that she supported them. While, at first glance, the location of the murder looks damning, the evidence is only circumstantial.

There is, in fact, another source contemporary to Ethelred, which seems to suggest the contention that Edward was killed by renegade noblemen, rather than by his stepmother.

In the 'Sermon of the Wolf' given by Archbishop Wulfstan of York between 1013 and 1016, which dwelt on the disasters that

England had suffered since the murder, the churchman mused that

> now too often a kinsman does not protect a kinsman any more than a stranger, neither a father his son, nor sometimes a son his own father, nor one brother against each other...
>
> It is the greatest of all treachery in the world that a man betray his lord's soul; and a full treachery in the world that a man should betray his lord to death, or drive him in his lifetime from the land; and both have happened in this country: Edward was betrayed and then killed, and afterward burnt, and Aethelred was driven out of his country.[32]

At worst, the sermon implies that Ethelred and his mother were guilty of not seeking to track down the murderers, rather than planning the deed themselves, since it appears to have been carried out by men who owed allegiance to the king. The Anglo-Saxon Chronicle also distinguishes between Edward's murderers and his kin in the statement that 'his earthly relatives would not avenge him'.[33] It has been suggested that this means only that Edward's kin, Elfrida and Ethelred, did not track down his murderers, and that they cannot be considered to have been the assassins themselves.[34] This statement is contained in the difficult-to-date E version of the Chronicle and follows a statement that the murder occurred at Corfe. It adds support to the view that the location of the murder, although damning, does not necessarily point to Elfrida's guilt. Her involvement is certainly possible, given the fact that it led to her taking on the powerful role of queen mother. However, she would have needed to be a skilful actress to have lulled Edward into such a sense of security that he was prepared to pay a social call to a woman who was planning his murder.

The increasing emphasis on Elfrida's role in the murder also appears to have its origins among those who were politically opposed to the queen. Goscelin of Saint-Bertin, for example, when writing his Life of St Edith based on traditions current at Wilton nunnery in the second half of the eleventh century, recorded that 'Edward, while out of pious affection he sought to see his brother Aethelred, came up against the sword wielded on behalf of his brother, and the assassinating dagger defeated the peaceful intentions of the two brothers; slain by the treachery of his stepmother'.[35] Elfrida was never going to be given the benefit of the doubt at Wilton, where the longevity of Wulfthryth meant that she was still remembered personally by some of the nuns when Goscelin came to write his history. It seems that Elfrida's attempts to take control of the nunneries during Edgar's reign left her unpopular with the nuns, who were only too happy to spread scurrilous stories about her. It has been pointed out that even her own foundation of Wherwell recorded that she was guilty of the murder, apparently welcoming Edward with a kiss before causing him to be stabbed while drinking.[36] The male house at Ely, of which she was a substantial benefactor, similarly blackened her name.[37] It cannot be discounted that Elfrida, known for her enthusiasm for reform, had made enemies in the religious houses who were determined to order themselves without outside interference. As a result, the later stories of her guilt cannot be considered in anyway unbiased.

Based on the evidence, Elfrida's guilt cannot be entirely disproved, but it must be considered to be highly doubtful. For Edward to have sought to visit her with only a few attendants suggests that the pair had made peace, and were on friendly terms. With the loss of many of his advisors at Calne he may have been seeking to further amend the agreement to ensure that Elfrida continued to support him while he stabilised his position. While Elfrida was prepared to make terms, it is clear that some of the men around her were not. Although the men involved in the murder are nowhere named in the sources, suspicion must fall on Ealdorman Elfhere, who is a plausible nobleman to have been staying with the queen, particularly if he knew that the king was due to arrive. Elfhere later took part in a very public act of atonement for the murder, which again suggests that it may have been him, rather than Elfrida, who was the driving force behind it. Elfhere's power and his importance to Elfrida, not to mention the fact that they were kin, would certainly be good reason for no action to be taken against the murderers, as well as the evidence to show that Elfrida and later her son hoped that the crime would quickly be forgotten.

At worst, the contemporary evidence suggests Elfrida, waiting inside the house, might have had some inkling that the gathering men meant the king harm. Even this is uncertain, however, given that the Life of St Oswald, which is a source favourable to Dunstan and his party, considered that the 'magnates had agreed among themselves a wicked plot', giving no indication that the queen was even aware of this.

Although Ethelred and Elfrida were the ultimate beneficiaries of the murder, in 978 this did not look immediately likely, and the crisis caused by Edward's assassination once again threatened to divide the kingdom and put it in a state of near civil war.

THE AFTERMATH OF THE MURDER

The murder of Edward the Martyr plunged England into confusion. While the ten-year-old Ethelred must always have seemed the most likely candidate, he was not, in fact, the only one. Additionally, both he and his mother had to contend with significant posthumous interest in Edward the Martyr, leaving Elfrida, initially, at a loss as to just how to deal with a murder committed by her own supporters.

Edward's murder caused uproar in Elfrida's house on the evening of 18 March 978. The queen, waiting inside, heard the shouts and cries of her servants and retainers and immediately sought to find out what had happened. In the chaos, the queen must have felt a mix of emotions. Her son, the young Ethelred, roused from his bed by the commotion, wept.

There is some evidence that Ethelred, who in 978 became the last male-line descendant of Alfred the Great, was never considered to be a very promising specimen. As a young child he was overshadowed by his brother, Edmund, which may not have been helped by an unfortunate incident at his baptism when, according to William of Malmesbury, the younger prince defecated in the font.

Dunstan, who was officiating, was not prepared to overlook this slight, even in a child who can only have been, at most, a few days old. In front of everyone assembled, he angrily exclaimed, 'By God and his mother, this will be a sorry fellow!'[1] As an adult, Ethelred had a complex relationship with his mother, but there are fewer details for his childhood. According to William of Malmesbury, who based his story on the *Passion of Edward the Martyr*, Ethelred rushed to Elfrida shortly after the murder, and 'he so irritated his furious mother by his weeping, that, not having a whip at hand, she beat the little innocent with some candles she had snatched up, nor did she desist till herself bedewed him, nearly lifeless, with her tears. On this account he dreaded candles, during the rest of his life, to such a degree that he would never suffer the light of them to be brought into his presence.'[2] The idea that Ethelred had a fear of candles seems laughable, and he would have had to endure many a dark night if this was the case. In reality, this story was intended to blacken Elfrida's name. Even if she had no love for her son, and there is no evidence to suggest that this was the case, he was still her greatest asset, and she would hardly have risked beating him to the point of unconsciousness.

The most immediate action required was to retrieve Edward's body, which had been carried away by his horse, dragging behind it on the ground. It was imperative that the body did not fall into the hands of Dunstan and his faction; Elfrida's immediate response to hearing of the king's death appears to have been her attempting to minimise the attention it gained, perhaps in the hope that it could be forgotten. According to Gaimar, Elfrida had the body hidden in reeds on a lonely moor near her house. She then, apparently, hid in her house when Edward's followers came to look for him, hoping that they would leave empty-handed.[3] Edward's supporters decided to look for his body, and were guided to it by a light shining onto it from heaven and miracles ocurring at the grave, and they took it to Shaftesbury, where he was honoured as a saint.[4] This story appears only in a post-Conquest source and seems to have been based on later ideas of Edward's sanctity. The idea of miracles occurring around Edward's tomb was just the sort of rumour Elfrida wanted to avoid, and probably explains the obscure burial that Edward received at Wareham.

Bryhtferth's Life of St Oswald provides the earliest in-depth source of information about Edward's burial at Wareham:

> The martyr of God was carried by the servants and brought to the house of a certain unimportant person; where no Gregorian harmony nor funeral dirge was heard, but so glorious a king of the whole land lay covered with a mean covering, waiting the light of the day.[5]

Once the king's body had been retrieved from where his horse had deposited it, Elfrida's followers decided to hide it away in an obscure place where it would not attract a cult – which would certainly have destabilised the rule of Edward's successor, even though it is unlikely that Ethelred or his mother were actually directly involved in the death. The body was taken to the house of an obscure thegn. No decision had yet been taken as to where it would be buried and, instead, it was kept covered up in the house, which must have felt rather macabre for the occupants. An attempt may also have been made to burn the body, in the hope of further hiding the remains. In his Sermon of the Wolf, Archbishop Wulfstan of York, who was alive at the time of the murder, claimed that 'Edward was betrayed and then killed, and afterwards burnt'.[6]

Although this is the only evidence that Edward's body was also burnt, it is just possible that there is a grain of truth in what the archbishop claimed. He was in a position to know. Furthermore it was the dishonour shown to the body that truly shocked the people of the time, rather than simply the murder itself. Political murder was one thing, but even King Athelstan, who had his half-brother Edwin drowned, saw that he was buried honourably in a church built for the dead man's soul.[7] He also did seven years' penance for the death, publicly atoning for his crime.[8]

By refusing even to make a show of avenging the death, and by denying Edward an honourable burial, Elfrida and the rest of Ethelred's supporters did not live up to the standards of morality expected in the late tenth century. They must soon have realised that they had made a terrible mistake in refusing to honour the dead king, who was slain, nominally at least, on Ethelred's behalf, although not on his or his mother's orders. The body's stay in the peasant's house was only temporary, with an obscure burial at Wareham quickly arranged. Even hiding the body overnight while decisions were made attracted publicity; a church dedicated to Edward at Corfe was later reportedly built on the site of the house.[9]

The Calne accident had already ensured that Edward was politically isolated, and Elfrida, caught off guard at Corfe, must have hoped that Ethelred would be accepted as king and that the murder would be forgotten. Certainly, if indeed the murderer was Elfhere, she could not have punished him. Edward's faction refused to die, however, and the queen was forced to spend over a year battling for the coronation of her son.

It is a measure of the continuing strength of Dunstan's party that, in the face of Ethelred's candidacy as the sole surviving Aetheling, his election was very far from being a foregone conclusion. Goscelin, in his Life of Edith, tells an interesting story that may well have been recalled by the nuns of Wilton from whom he drew his source material. According to the *Life,* soon after the murder, Edward's supporters, still intending to reject Ethelred, came together to decide upon an alternative successor.[10] Without any male heir, their thoughts turned to Edgar's other surviving child and 'they all agreed to take St Edith from the monastery and elevate her to her father's throne – for women rule among many nations – believing indeed that a lady of mature foresight could govern so great a kingdom better than childish ignorance'. This was not such a crazy suggestion as it first appears. Eadgifu had shown that a woman could wield power, as had Elfrida herself. Additionally, although it was Edith's royal blood that could secure the throne, it would have been intended that she would marry a nobleman of Dunstan's party's choosing, which would effectively allow them to choose their own king from among their number. Ethelflaed, the daughter of Alfred the Great, had ruled Mercia following her husband's death, and had attempted to pass that kingdom on to her daughter on her own death. Female rule was therefore not impossible. It was problematic, however, particularly since Edith's sex precluded her from being an Aetheling and, thus, actually throneworthy. Nonetheless, as the popularity of Matilda of Scotland's marriage to Henry I showed in 1100, in England women were known to be able to transmit royal blood and, potentially, a claim to the throne. Matilda was widely seen as an heir to the Anglo-Saxon kings through her mother, St Margaret, who was a great-granddaughter of Ethelred II.

Once they had resolved upon their candidate, Ethelred's opponents went in person to Wilton to see Edith. According to her Life, she was reluctant – perhaps at hearing that she was to be forced to marry. The meeting grew increasingly heated and the party 'surrounded her, urged her, begged her, raised their voices, finally indicated that they would use force'. Edith was not about to commit herself to such a hostile assembly who were, after all, the party of her elder half-brother rather than herself or her maternal family. Although the delay in Ethelred's coronation suggests that attempts were made to negotiate with Edith for some time, she always refused, presumably to her stepmother's relief.

The attempt to crown Edith or, most likely, her husband, was built on public revulsion to the murder. The Anglo-Saxon Chronicle entry in version E shows some of the strength of feeling surrounding Edward's death. According to the Chronicle,

> no worse deed for the English race was done than this was, since they first sought out the land of Britain. Men murdered him, but God exalted him. In life he was an earthly king; after death he is now a heavenly saint. His earthly relatives would not avenge him, but his Heavenly Father has much avenged him. Those earthly slayers wanted to destroy his memory upon earth, but the sublime avenger has spread abroad his memory in the heavens and on earth. Those who either would not bow to his living body, those men humbly bow the knees to his dead bones.[11]

This emotional response was unexpected, and Elfrida must have been horrified by the cult that rapidly grew up around her dead stepson and the impact this had on her son's candidacy. According to several sources, miracles were quickly reported at Edward's resting place at Wareham, including cures for lameness, dumbness and sickness.[12] Lights were said to shine on his grave from the sky, a sign seen by the majority as a token of sanctity.[13]

William of Malmesbury had heard that Elfrida was worried enough by the reports to attempt to go to Edward's humble grave herself:

The news telling what the martyr had done spread through England. His murderess was worried and attempted to go to his grave. But the animal which usually carried her and which had always been quicker than the wind, outstripping the breezes themselves, as the saying goes, now at God's command stood motionless. Her servants attacked it with whips, but their efforts were in vain. She changed animals, but the same thing happened.[14]

Again, this is part of the dark legend that grew up around Elfrida and no pre-Conquest source confirms the claims about the queen's troublesome mounts. It is, however, certainly possible that she took steps to disprove the growing cult herself: the first wife of her son's successor, Cnut, did just that when she was Regent of Norway and faced with claims of sanctity in relation to the former king there. This later queen was singularly unsuccessful, and so was Elfrida. Her party were, however, able to negotiate with Dunstan, who must have been aware that, without Edward or Edith, he had no one left to crown, except Ethelred.

The reconciliation occurred in 979 when, according to the Anglo-Saxon Chronicle, Ealdorman Elfhere took Edward's body from Wareham to Shaftesbury where it was, at last, honourably buried.[15] According to tradition, the body was found to be undecayed, which was expected in the tenth century of a saint.[16] The party set out from Wareham on 13 February, in deepest winter, spending a week on the road due to poor conditions, before gratefully arriving at their destination on 20 February.[17] Shaftesbury, as the resting place of his grandmother, St Elfgifu, and also, probably, the home of his own mother, was a suitable place for the young king to lie, and one that satisfied the need for him to be honourably interred. The reburial ceremony was attended by Ealdorman Elfhere, Dunstan and Edith, Edward's sister, although Elfrida stayed away. It was a grand affair, which must have been particularly uncomfortable for Elfhere. According to the Life of St Oswald,

the renowned ealdorman Aelfhere came with a multitude of people, and ordered his body to be lifted up from the earth; and when this was done and the body uncovered, they found and saw him as whole from every stain or pollution as he was in the beginning. Seeing this, all were amazed, rejoicing with exultation in the lord, who alone does wonderful things in the word. The servants then washed the body of the reverend king, and placed it, clothed in new vestments, in a coffin or shrine and noble thegns with the bier placed on their shoulders carried him to the place in which they buried him honourably, where masses and sacred oblations were celebrated for the redemption of his soul, by the ealdorman's orders.[18]

Elfhere's actions represent a new policy of reconciliation designed to knit together the factions in England behind Ethelred, and can probably be seen as an act of penance by the murderer himself. Certainly, Princess Edith also attended from Wilton, again suggesting an acceptance of Ethelred as king.[19] Much of the criticism of Ethelred and his mother was centred on the fact that the king was neither avenged nor given an honourable burial and, although she could not easily avenge the murder, Elfrida could, at least, provide him with an appropriate resting place. With the translation completed, Elfrida, who was Ethelred's closest advisor, arranged his coronation ceremony.[20]

Edward's reburial was Dunstan's price for crowning Ethelred and, on 14 April 979, he was finally crowned by both Dunstan and Archbishop Oswald at Kingston.[21] Elfrida watched the coronation proudly from her seat of honour, considering it the fulfilment of her ambitions. The eleven-year-old Ethelred, in spite of his youth, acquitted himself well, showing the assembly 'fascinating manners, handsome countenance, and graceful appearance'.[22] He was received with 'great rejoicing' at the coronation – probably by a populace relieved to finally have a king again, even if he was a child.[23] Ethelred, for all his faults, inherited the good looks of both his parents and knew instinctively how to make himself attractive to a crowd. There is no contemporary evidence that anything was amiss at the ceremony, and later reports that Dunstan prophesied the young king's doom are unlikely.[24] William of Malmesbury's claim that Dunstan had no wish to crown Ethelred and did so only in very bad grace is considerably more plausible, although a sulky archbishop is unlikely to have overshadowed the day for Elfrida.[25] Claims that the coronation was followed by a strange cloud that was seen throughout the whole of England can probably also be dismissed.[26]

The coronation was the culmination of all Elfrida's ambitions and, after more than three years in the shade, she was back in power as one of the leading figures at the royal court. In the days following the coronation, she was busy organising the government through which she would rule during Ethelred's minority. The role of queen mother was the most powerful political opening for a woman in Anglo-Saxon England and, in 979, it was Elfrida's.

I I

ETHELRED'S MINORITY

Ethelred could not have been more than twelve years old at the time of his accession.[1] He was at least three or four years away from political maturity and some sort of regency was required. Elfrida, as a crowned queen and the young king's mother, was in the best position to take this role for herself.

There was no precedent for a child king in recent Wessex history. Both Eadwig and Edgar, the only other young kings, were both in their mid- to late teens and appear to have been considered fully fit to rule, as was Edward the Martyr. Ethelred, on the other hand, was certainly not politically mature. No direct details survive concerning the regency arrangements but, although a fiction was maintained that he ruled alone, a regency council would have been in place. Elfrida and Bishop Ethelwold took the main places, as well as seeking to reward their own supporters, such as Ealdorman Elfhere and Elfrida's brother, Ordulf, who returned to court in the early years of his nephew's reign.

Although the role of queen mother was invariably powerful, the only known Anglo-Saxon precedent for a queen officially taking the role of regent for a minor is Elfgifu of Northampton, the first wife of Cnut, who was sent to Norway in 1029 to rule on behalf of her young son, Sweyn.[2] Elfgifu acted in her son's name, but it was clear to all in Norway who was behind the new regime: 'Elfgifu's time' is, even to this day, remembered as a time of oppression and disaster.[3] Clearly, she made her authority felt in Norway, introducing a number of unpopular new laws.

Elfrida fulfilled a similar role to Elfgifu of Northampton. She appears regularly in Ethelred's charters between 979 and 984, demonstrating that she regularly attended councils during his minority.[4] She also generally witnessed as *mater regis,* or 'king's mother', something that, as with Eadgifu, is suggestive of what she saw as the source of her power. Elfrida also appeared in a number of Edgar's charters, but it was in the early years of Ethelred's reign that she reached the height of her power. During the first few years of Ethelred's reign she appears in ten surviving charters, a high number for an Anglo-Saxon queen.[5] She is high on the witness list in these charters, another indication of status at the Anglo-Saxon court. In a charter granting land in 983, for example, Elfrida witnessed below the king and bishops but appears as 'Aelfthryth Regina'.[6] This low placing was a rare aberration in Ethelred's minority and, generally, her status was higher. In two New Minster charters, for example, she witnessed as the king's mother, directly behind her son.[7] It may particularly have pleased Elfrida that the third witness on both of these charters, displaying lower status than herself, was Dunstan. Dunstan had generally been the second witness behind Edgar and Edward the Martyr, and this demotion of his status behind the queen cannot have been easy for him to stomach. He always witnessed before her when the pair both attended councils during Edgar's reign.

Elfrida was not the only person who had campaigned for Ethelred's accession, and his other supporters expected to be given important roles in any regency council.[8] Ealdorman Elfhere appears as the most prominent ealdorman on the witness list of Ethelred's charters until his death in 983.[9] The other major supporter of Ethelred was Bishop Ethelwold himself. Like Elfthryth, Ethelwold appears regularly in the charters of Ethelred's minority and was clearly in regular attendance at royal councils. He always witnessed below the Archbishops Dunstan and Oswald,[10] but this should not be taken as a measure of the three bishops' actual standing: Ethelwold, as Bishop of Winchester, could not realistically place himself above his two ecclesiastical superiors and he could not obtain promotion while the other two lived. Elfrida was therefore forced to accept Dunstan's continued presence at court although, politically, he appears to have become almost a nonentity with Ethelred's accession.[11] The queen had always represented the anti-Dunstan faction at court and she and her supporters worked actively to ensure that he had no role in the regency regime. Evidence of the queen's favour to her two supporters is clear from the fact that Ethelred made a grant of land to Bishop Ethelwold on the very day of his coronation.[12] Another early charter of the young king granted land to both Ethelwold and Ealdorman Elfhere, and it is difficult not to see these grants as rewards given by Elfrida to Ethelred's greatest supporters.

Ethelwold and Elfrida both wished to re-ignite the religious reform in England and quickly turned their policy towards the Church. Ethelwold had been busy rebuilding the Old Minster church for some years and, in 980, it was finally ready for dedication.[13] Elfrida and Ethelred moved the court to Winchester to attend the ceremony. This was a major ceremonial occasion and has been suggested to have been used as another reconciliation gesture by the supporters of Ethelred towards the supporters of Edward the Martyr.[14] The ceremonies lasted for two days, beginning on 20 October, and were attended by Dunstan, as well as seven other bishops.[15] Both Elfrida and Ethelwold must have hoped that this would be the first of many such occasions during Ethelred's reign and religious foundations continued to be made, including monasteries at Cerne and Eynsham.[16] Sherborne Cathedral also had its secular clerks expelled in the early 990s and Canterbury went through the same process a few years later.[17]

Elfrida had been a prominent supporter and benefactress of the Church throughout Edgar's reign, and it seems likely that she had always nursed ambition to found her own religious houses, as her mentor Ethelwold had done. She began to prepare for her foundation at Wherwell soon after Ethelred's accession.[18] Wherwell was part of the see of Winchester and the location of Elfrida's nunnery was probably chosen based on Ethelwold's advice. Certainly, the nunnery's endowment included estates donated from the New Minster, Winchester, and the bishop's help would have been required.[19] Interestingly, Wherwell had also been the home of Wenflaed, the aunt of Wulfhild and Wulfthryth, who had assisted Edgar in his courtships. As seems likely, this lady, who had taken religious vows, was also Edgar's grandmother and, perhaps, any ladies remaining in the town from Wenflaed's religious community remained friendly towards the queen.

Elfrida took an active interest in the foundation of her nunnery at Wherwell and also her second nunnery at Amesbury, intending them to be her legacy.[20] She was later described as 'diligently building up' Wherwell in a charter of her son, suggesting she oversaw the foundation herself.[21] There is less evidence for her involvement with Amesbury, although evidence suggests that both houses originally shared an abbess, implying strong links between them.[22] Several medieval writers believed that there was a darker motive behind her actions. According to William of Malmesbury,

> we know that Wherwell was built in honour of the Holy Cross by Aelfthryth, wife of King Edgar, in her compunction for the cruel death of her stepson, Edward, whose confidante and patron she had been.[23]

This speaks more of the generally poor relationship Elfrida had with the nunneries since even her own foundations found little positive to say about her. Other post-Conquest writers claimed that Wherwell was founded from remorse for the death of her first husband, a crime that does not appear to have even occurred, let alone been carried out by the queen. There was nothing unusual about a queen founding a nunnery. Edgar's mother, St Elfgifu, was reputed to have refounded the nunnery at Shaftesbury.[24] Similarly, the later Edith Godwin rebuilt the nunnery at Wilton in stone during her queenship.[25] Eahlswith, the widow of Alfred the Great, founded the Nunnaminster convent at Winchester during her widowhood, another indication that the foundation of religious houses was an acceptable outlet for the time and energies of royal widows.[26] Elfrida's reputation just got worse and worse and, by the twelfth century, her *obit* was not even celebrated at Wherwell, her own foundation.[27]

Ethelred had been around twelve at his accession in 978 and, ordinarily, could have been expected to attain his majority at the age of around fifteen or sixteen, as his uncle, King Eadwig, had. Ethelred, however, was still under the control of Elfrida and Ethelwold by the time of his fifteenth birthday and, also, his sixteenth, and neither his mother nor the bishop showed any intention of releasing their grip on power once the king was an adult. It seems likely that, having ruled together for several years, neither Elfrida nor Ethelwold relished relinquishing power to a king whom both still considered a boy and they may have reasoned that, at fifteen, he was still not old enough to truly rule the country. Both must have enjoyed the freedom that their regency gave them and they probably reasoned that it would be better for Ethelred if they waited before handing power over to him.

This is not a view that found much support with Ethelred himself. By the time he reached fifteen or sixteen, he had come to resent the power that his mother and the bishop had over him. He did not have that long to wait and, by the early 980s, the older generation at court had begun to die out. Elfhere died in 983 and his death opened up the way for the appointment of a new man in his place. Even Ethelred's half-sister, Edith, who retained some political influence in the new reign, died in 984 after a short illness in which 'pain gripped her virginal body and wasted it away'. She was comforted by her mother and Dunstan, who both must have been aware that they lost considerable political leverage with her death, even if she was quickly reputed to be a saint.[28] Wulfthryth, Elfrida's old rival, was devastated by the death of her only child, spending long years at Wilton and dying only 'after a long martyrdom of bereavement and heavenly desire'.[29] Much of the vitriol directed at Elfrida from the nunneries may have come from her.

The most significant death came on 1 August 984 and was that of Bishop Ethelwold himself.[30] The bishop had worn himself out through his austere lifestyle and his death may have been expected for some time. Throughout his life he had shown scant regard for his own health; for example, during the refoundation of the monastery at Abingdon, 'while he was working on the building, a huge post fell on him and threw him down into a pit and broke nearly all his ribs on one side; and if the pit had not received him, he would have been completely crushed'.[31] With accidents such as this and even attempted poisonings, it is perhaps no surprise that Ethelwold 'was often afflicted with illness in his bowels and legs, spending sleepless nights from pain, and nevertheless going about by day as if well, though pale'.[32] Even the austere Ethelwold realised eventually that he needed to make allowances for his health and, during his final illness, consented to eat meat at Dunstan's command.[33]

News of the death grieved Elfrida. He had been her closest ally for the past twenty years and she felt both empty and lost without him. She may, perhaps, have attended his burial at the Old Minster. She would certainly have considered it fitting that he was buried in the very church that he had spent years rebuilding. She was gratified to hear that, within only a short time, there were reports of miracles at his tomb.[34] By the mid-990s he was actively commemorated as a saint, something that the queen heartily condoned.

Elfrida's feelings of bewilderment increased when Ethelred, released from Ethelwold's control for the first time in his life, seized the moment to move against his mother and send her away from court, plunging her into political obscurity.[35]

12

ELFRIDA'S OBSCURITY

The death of Bishop Ethelwold ushered in a major change in the English court and also the lives of Ethelred and Elfrida. By the end of 984, Elfrida had ceased to attend council meetings, retiring to her own estates. The period between 984 and 993 was the most obscure in her queenship, and also one of the most turbulent periods in English history.

Although there is no direct evidence about why Elfrida left court in 984, it is clear that Ethelwold's death marked a major change in her life and her relationship with her son. The loss of the bishop is generally seen as Ethelred's cue to become independent from his mother, and policies after 984 suggest that he had been irked by the dominance of Elfrida and Ethelwold.[1] With the death of the aged and somewhat terrifying bishop, it was possible for the young king to assert himself against his mother.

Although no details of Elfrida's fall from power in 984 survive, a detailed account of another Anglo-Saxon queen, Emma of Normandy, does survive, and is a useful parallel in determining just what happened in 984. Emma, who was the widow of both Ethelred II and Cnut, helped engineer the accession of Edward the

Confessor, the son of her first marriage, after the death of King Harthacnut, the son of her second marriage. Her eldest son, who by the time of his accession was approaching middle age and had spent much of his time in exile, was far from grateful and resented attempts by Emma to be the power behind the throne as she had been under Harthacnut. Edward moved against his overbearing mother quickly. According to the Anglo-Saxon Chronicle,

> here Edward was consecrated as king at Winchester on the first day of Easter. And that year, fourteen days before St Andrew's Day, the king was so counselled that he and Earl Leofric and Earl Godwin and Earl Siward and their band rode from Gloucester to Winchester, on the Lady [Emma] by surprise, and robbed her of all the treasures which she owned, which were untold, because earlier she was very hard on the king her son, in that she did less for him than he wanted before he became king, and also afterwards; and they let her stay inside afterwards.[2]

The key to removing Emma's influence at court was to deprive her of her treasures, something which Edward recognised. According to the entry for 1043 in the 'E' version of the Chronicle, he was thorough in his approach, since he brought 'into his hands all the lands which his mother owned, and took from her all she owned in gold and silver and in untold things, because earlier she had kept it from him too firmly'.[3] Edward later took similar action against his own wife when she lost his favour. In 1053, when he attempted to divorce his queen, Edith Godwin, by forcibly retiring her to Wherwell Abbey, he also despoiled her of her lands, as is clear from the 'E' version of the Chronicle's entry for 1052, which states that Edward was compelled to restore Edith to all her property after the return of her powerful family from exile.[4] Clearly, Edward the Confessor knew the importance of neutralising a powerful queen through the removal of her property and his father, Ethelred, presumably did too.

Although there is no firm evidence that Elfrida was forcibly removed from court and despoiled of her property, the evidence of other Anglo-Saxon queens seems to suggest that she would have been. She had been granted a large number of estates by Edgar and was a major landowner in her own right with estates spread across southern England.[5] This wealth represented a formidable challenge to Ethelred's authority and Elfrida's estates were probably the first thing he attempted to reclaim when she was knocked from power in 984. Elfrida appears to have made only rare visits, if she made any at all, to the court between 984 and 993 and attests no surviving charters during that period, suggesting that she was kept firmly away from council meetings and other aspects of the government.[6]

Ethelred relished the freedom that the death of Ethelwold and the exile of his mother brought, and 984 marked a major change in royal policy. According to Ethelred himself, the death of Ethelwold deprived the country of a man 'whose industry and pastoral care administered not only to my interest but also to that of all inhabitants of this country, the common people as well as the leading men'.[7] These words were spoken by the king in 993 after he had come to regret his rebellion in 984, but they demonstrate his inability to select new councillors of the calibre of Ethelwold and Elfrida. In the same charter, Ethelred concluded that things went wrong in England after the death of the bishop due to his own youthful ignorance and the greed displayed by those around him.[8] Elfrida's son was unable to select reliable advisors during the period between 984 and 993 and this has contributed to his nickname, 'Ethelred the Unready' – a pun on the king's own name, which means 'noble counsel'.[9] 'Unraed', from which 'Unready' developed, translates as 'no counsel', giving a literal translation of Ethelred's name as 'noble counsel, no counsel'.[10] This was clearly an unflattering description and one intended to convey a picture of the king's stupidity.

The main aspect of Ethelred's policy between 984 and 993 that would have displeased Elfrida was her son's attitude towards the Church. She had raised him to be favourable to the reformed Church and she must have been horrified to see that, in 984, he was simply prepared to abandon the principles that she had instilled in him. Ethelred had, apparently, been nursing a resentment towards the Church as well as towards Ethelwold and Elfrida during his minority. He resented the loss of royal lands in gifts to the monasteries and resolved that, when he had finally asserted himself as ruler, he would act to restore as much property to the Crown as he could.[11] His mother, who had been involved in persuading Edgar to make many of these grants, cannot but have been furious at his reaction against the reform movement and, given her forceful character, she made sure that everyone knew of her disgust. This may account for the rumours that she had retired voluntarily in dismay at Ethelred's kingship.

The entry for 986 in the Anglo-Saxon Chronicle states that 'here the king did for the bishopric at Rochester; and here the great pestilence among cattle first came to England'.[12] It is the first part of this entry that is significant to Ethelred's assertion of his authority in the mid-980s although the Chronicle gives few details of what actually occurred at Rochester. It is therefore necessary to turn to Florence of Worcester for a fuller description of the king's actions towards Rochester in 986:

Aethelred, king of England, on account of some quarrel, laid siege to the city of Rochester, but seeing that it would be difficult to reduce it, retired in wrath, and laid waste the lands of [the church of] St Andrew the Apostle.[13]

Although no details of the quarrel survive, it seems probable that it involved Ethelred's attempts to recover royal land that had been given to the see during the reign of his father. Certainly, he was party to the appropriation of lands belonging to Rochester in the late 980s or early 990s. The attack should be seen as an attempt to forcibly wrest control of the lands from the bishopric. Lands were restored to Rochester by Ethelred in 995 and 998 and, in both charters, he adopted a apologetic tone, suggesting that he had been one of the prime movers behind the appropriation of the estates.[14]

Attacks on the Church did not stop with Rochester. According to another apologetic charter of the 990s, at some point between 984 and 993 the Bishop of Ramsey and Ealdorman Elfric persuaded Ethelred to reduce the liberties of Abingdon Abbey and also to sell the Abbey of Abingdon itself to Elfric's brother.[15] The king also confiscated estates belonging to the abbey at the same time, which he restored later, full of remorse.[16] Abingdon Abbey had been rebuilt from a ruin by Ethelwold during the reign of King Eadred, and it is possible that the king saw an attack on Abingdon as a convenient way to attack the memory of the bishop who had dominated his life for so long. Certainly, an attack on Abingdon must have been interpreted as an attack on the reform and it is something of which Elfrida could never approve. Ethelred also attacked the Old Minster itself, a religious establishment that was again intimately associated with Bishop Ethelwold. Although no details of the attacks on the Old Minster survive, in 997 he felt guilty enough to restore a number of estates to the church that he had earlier appropriated.[17]

Watching her son's actions from afar, Elfrida must have deeply resented her exile, although others at court, such as Archbishop Dunstan, relished her fall from power. Dunstan, although never prominent during Ethelred's reign, did retain a presence at court. He benefited slightly from the queen's removal and was able to regain his position as a witness to charters second only to the king. For example, in a charter of 987 in which Ethelred granted land at Maningford Abbots in Wiltshire to a certain Ethelwold, Dunstan was able to assert himself enough to witness directly after the king while Elfrida did not appear at all.[18] She cannot have been pleased to cede her place to Dunstan of all people and she was not displeased to hear of his death on 19 May 988.[19] Dunstan and Elfrida were locked in rivalry with each other for over twenty years, but while she cannot have lamented the death, it could not have escaped her that the ranks of the people she had known at court were thinning and that she was increasingly part of a past generation. This feeling was reinforced when Archbishop Oswald died a few years later, the last of the great reforming churchmen.

If Elfrida had a sense during the late 980s and early 990s that her generation was dying out, these feelings cannot have been alleviated by the news from court that Ethelred had taken a wife. The date of the marriage is not recorded but it must have been by around the mid-980s, as in 993 his four eldest sons attest a charter at court.[20] Given that Elfrida was unlikely to tolerate another queen at court, the marriage probably occurred after her exile and without her consent.

Ethelred's first wife is mentioned in no contemporary sources and attests no known charters.[21] In fact, her existence can only be glimpsed by the fact that, by 993, the king was the father of four sons; Athelstan, Ecgberht, Eadred and Edmund.[22] A fifth son, Eadwig, also began to attest charters in 997 and a sixth, Edgar, in 1001. Two daughters, Elfgifu and Edith, are known. Ethelred's wife was obviously fully occupied in childbearing throughout her marriage, and all that is known for certain is that she was still alive at least into the late 990s and that she was either dead, or repudiated, by 1002 when Ethelred married again.

Given the obscurity surrounding Ethelred's first wife, it is not surprising that there is a great deal of confusion concerning her and it has even been suggested that the king may have been married twice before 1002, something that cannot be discounted.[23] Since no contemporary sources name Ethelred's wife (or wives), it is necessary to turn to later accounts for details concerning her. According to some reports, she was called Elfgifu and was a daughter of an ealdorman called Ethelberht. According to others, she was the daughter of Ealdorman Thored of York.[24] No Ealdorman Ethelberht is known to have existed at this time. Ealdorman Thored, on the other hand, certainly did exist, although he ceases to appear in the sources after 992 and, by 993, his ealdordom had been passed on to another man.[25] This coincides with the return of Elfrida to court, and it is possible that she may have been involved in the neutralisation of Thored. She certainly totally overshadowed his daughter, who attests no charters, suggesting that she did not attend the royal council. Even in exile Elfrida, as an anointed queen, commanded authority and her daughter-in-law was entirely unable to supplant her.

Elfrida's role as a consecrated queen also meant that, although there was clearly some estrangement between her and her son during the late 980s and early 990s, Ethelred still trusted his mother enough to place the upbringing of his family in her hands rather than those of his wife. Eadgifu had supervised the upbringing of Edgar and Eadwig, and Elfrida took a similar role, including identifying suitable foster parents and arranging their education. Her grandson, Athelstan, was fostered by a woman named Elfswith who, 'because of her great deserts', received a large legacy in the prince's Will. Elfrida may, perhaps, have kept the girls with her or placed them in a nunnery as she had done with her own stepdaughter, Ethelflaed. One of Elfrida's granddaughters was later Abbess of Wherwell, suggesting that she may have been raised there. If so, she would have spent considerable time with her grandmother when the elder woman retired there in her old age. Elfrida may well have seen her possession of the royal heirs as her route back to court. Although she was not responsible for their day-to-day care, the children were fond of her. In 1014, when Elfrida was long since dead, her grandson, Athelstan, remembered her fondly in his Will, giving testimony to the strength of his feelings towards his grandmother:

> I now declare that all those things which I have granted to God, to God's church and God's servants, are done for the soul of my dear father, King Aethelred, and for mine, and for the soul of Aelfthryth, my grandmother, who brought me up.[26]

Elfrida was granted the estate of Dean in Sussex when she accepted the charge of her grandchildren.[27] This had traditionally belonged to the Aethelings in Anglo-Saxon England and she would have spent some of her time there with the children. When they were with her, her household would have been greatly expanded, with the young princes requiring their own sword polishers, stag huntsmen and seneschals to ensure that they were able to live as befitted their status.[28] The boys also brought considerable material wealth with them. At the time of his death, Athelstan possessed a sword that had belonged to the famous King Offa, as well as a silver-coated trumpet and a gold crucifix, among other fine objects. It was Elfrida's role to fit them for their future as princes and, perhaps, kings.

If Elfrida had hoped when she accepted the charge of her grandchildren that they would provide her with a return to court, she was correct. At Pentecost in 993 Elfrida reappeared at a royal council at Winchester in the company of the older Aethelings.[29] She had been absent from court for nine years and was grateful of the chance to return to the seat of power. Ethelred also seems to have been glad of the return of his mother, since the court of the 990s was a very different one from the one that Elfrida had presided over in the late 970s and early 980s. For the first time in over half a century, England was faced by a threat from across the seas.

13

THE RETURN OF THE VIKINGS

Ethelred's reign is chiefly remembered for the return of the Vikings to England. These attacks by Scandinavian raiders had largely ceased by the end of the ninth century. In 980 the peace was shattered when a Viking raiding army arrived at Southampton and ravaged the settlement there.[1] It was the start of one of the most devastating periods in English history.

The first Viking attack in 980 was during Elfrida's period of regency and she must have been informed immediately of the new threat, ordering that the coastal settlements be on their guard against future attacks. The attack quickly proved not be isolated, with a raid on Padstow in 981 and then attacks all along the south coast.[2] The following year Elfrida and the rest of Ethelred's council were shocked to hear that London, one of the country's principal settlements, had been burned.[3] In the 980s the raids were still small-scale and sporadic, but they soon increased in scope and ambition.

Edgar and Elfrida's choice of the name Ethelred for their second son proved unfortunately prophetic, and the people of late tenth-century England were uncomfortably reminded of the reigns of Alfred the Great and his elder brother, Ethelred I, who were plagued by raiders intent on conquest. In 865, the very year that Ethelred I had succeeded to the throne, a great Viking army landed in England and spent the winter in East Anglia, marking the beginning of an attempt to conquer the kingdom of Wessex.[4] Ethelred I's namesake, Elfrida's own son, was similarly plagued with raiders looking to settle in his wealthy and hitherto peaceful kingdom.

The Viking raids continued into the 990s and it became clear that they were there to stay. In 991 ninety-three Viking ships arrived off the coast of England and raided first around Folkestone before travelling on to Sandwich and Ipswich.[5] The sight was terrifying, with the best surviving description of a Viking fleet, in the eleventh-century *Encomium Emmae Reginae*, declaring that

> so great, also, was the ornamentation of the ships, that the eyes of the beholders were dazzled and to those looking from afar they seemed of flame rather than of wood. For if at any time the sun cast the splendour of its rays amongst them, the flashing of arms shone in one place, in another the flame of suspended shields. Gold shone on the prows, silver also flashed on the variously shaped ships. So great, in fact, was the magnificence of the fleet, that if its lord had desired to conquer any people, the ships alone would have terrified the enemy, before the warriors whom they carried joined battle at all. For who could look upon the lions of the foe, terrible with the brightness of gold, who upon the men of metal, menacing with golden face, who upon the dragons burning with pure gold, without feeling any fear for the king of such a force? Furthermore, in this great expedition there was present no slave, no man freed from slavery, no low-born man, no man weakened by age; for all were noble, all strong with the might of mature age, all

sufficiently fit for any type of fighting, all of such great fleetness, that they scorned the speed of horsemen.[6]

This description refers to the Viking fleet commanded by Cnut in 1015, but it is likely that the Viking fleets of the late tenth century fitted a similar description. The raids themselves were no less terrifying, where the raiders 'fell upon a part of the country, seized booty, attacked and destroyed villages, overcame the enemies who met him, captured many of them, and at length returned to his comrades victorious with the spoil'.[7] The violence of such raids and their destructiveness profoundly shocked the people of England, who were used to the peace of Edgar's reign.

The Vikings focussed many of their attacks on the reformed religious establishments, which were, of course, newly wealthy. This was a particular source of grief to Elfrida, who had worked so hard to increase the prosperity of the Church. According to William of Malmesbury, Vikings burst into the church at Malmesbury Abbey, only to find that most of the treasures housed there had already been removed by the monks to safety.[8] The large shrine of St Aldhelm had proved impossible to dismantle, with the monks reasoning that the saint 'would protect it, if he wished. Alternatively, he could allow himself to become a laughing stock.'[9] St Aldhem did not wish to become a laughing stock and when a Viking attempted to cut the jewels from the shrine he was knocked down unconscious by the saint. Terrified by this, the Vikings fled, leaving the shrine intact. The Viking attack on Malmesbury shows something of the violence of the raids but, unfortunately, not all raids had quite such a happy ending.

The Viking fleet of 991 took the appearance more of an organised army than a band of opportunistic raiders.[10] It was also comparable in size to the ninth-century Viking Great Army that Alfred the Great had faced and there must have been at least 2,000 Vikings present in Ethelred's kingdom.[11] While the king and his advisors discussed how to respond, the Viking army entered the Blackwater estuary and took possession of Northey Island.[12] During August 991, an English army, led by Byrhtnoth, Ealdorman of Essex, who was the brother-in-law of Edgar's stepmother, Ethelflaed of Damerham, arrived at nearby Maldon and gave battle there with the Vikings. This battle caught the imagination of the English and inspired an epic poem praising the valour of Byrhtnoth and his men and, essentially, portraying the English action as a heroic last stand, with the 'stout-hearted warriors' standing firm in the face of peril.[13] Byrhtnoth, in particular, was portrayed as a valiant warrior, fighting on even when wounded. Finally, the earl's hand was smashed to pieces by a Viking blow but he still urged on his troops as he lay dying. The ealdorman's stand was, however, ultimately in vain and both he and most of his men were killed in an encounter that proved to be an important Viking victory. The poem was also intended as a reproach to Ethelred and his government for their inactivity, with Byrhtnoth referred to as 'one who intends to save this fatherland, Ethelred's kingdom'.[14]

After the Viking's victory at Maldon, the raiding fleet spent four months travelling around southern England, forcing local leaders to buy peace from them.[15] Paying the Vikings for peace was an established practise in England, with the intention being that the Vikings would then move on to another place to raid. This policy did not, however, always have the desired effect, as an example from Kent in 864 shows:

In the year of the Lord's Incarnation 864, the Vikings spent the winter on the Isle of Thanet, and concluded a firm treaty with the men of Kent. The men of Kent undertook to give them money to ensure that the treaty was kept. Meanwhile, however, the Vikings, like crafty foxes, secretly burst out of their camp by night, broke the treaty and, spurning the promise of money (for they knew they could get more money from stolen booty than from peace), laid waste to the entire eastern district of Kent.[16]

In this case, the Vikings did not actually accept the money, instead preferring to plunder it. What the people of late tenth-century England found more often, however, was that the Vikings were quite prepared to take the money but would return, regardless of their promises, soon after, seeking more. In spite of this, Ethelred had resolved to pay the Vikings tribute (or 'Danegeld') by the end of 991.

Ethelred is chiefly remembered for his attempts to pay off the Vikings with Danegeld payments and this appears to have been yet another policy on which he was badly advised. He held a number of council meetings at court once word had arrived of the defeat at Maldon. According to William of Malmesbury, a solution was finally suggested by the Archbishop of Canterbury, who suggested 'that money should repel them whom the sword could not; so a payment of ten thousand pounds satisfied the avarice of the Danes'.[17] Ethelred's council were demoralised by news of the heavy defeat at Maldon and believed that the Vikings were invincible. The king immediately set about organising a tax to provide funds for the payment, as well as sending an embassy to the Vikings to secure their agreement to leave following a payment of £10,000.[18] Ethelred must have waited anxiously for news that the Vikings had accepted the payment and would have been relieved when the fleet sailed away.

Ethelred's payment to the Vikings in 991 was not as naive as it may first seem. The king was clearly under no illusions that it would mean the end of the Viking raids. Early the following year, amid reports that a raiding army still remained within England, he ordered a royal fleet to be built in the hope of entrapping his enemy and, perhaps, obtaining a victory on the same scale as Alfred the Great at Edington, a battle that had brought the ninth-century Viking threat to an end. Once again, however, Ethelred found himself less well advised than his great-great-grandfather had been and his plans to defeat the Vikings through a military campaign were betrayed. According to the Anglo-Saxon Chronicle for 992,

> here the king and all his councillors decided that all the ships that were worth anything should be gathered to London town, in order that it should be attempted to entrap the raiding-army somewhere outside. But Ealdorman Aelfric, one of those to whom the king had most trust, ordered the raiding-army to be warned; and on the night before the morning on which they should have come together, this same Aelfric scurried away from the army, and then the raiding-army escaped.[19]

With advisors like Ealdorman Elfric and Archbishop Sigeric, who first suggested the Danegeld, it is no wonder that Ethelred recalled his mother to court in 993. By then, rather than remembering the irksome nature of his minority under Elfrida and Ethelwold, he had probably begun to look back at the early 980s as a time of peace and tranquillity. Elfrida was, by the 990s, elderly for the time. Like the rest of the king's advisors, she was at a loss as to how to respond to the threat. She was never able to regain the influence that she had previously held.

Ethelred's attempts to fight the Vikings in 992 had ended in failure due to the treachery of one of his own advisors and that, coupled with the memory of the heavy defeat at Maldon, gave the Vikings a popular reputation for invincibility. When a large Viking fleet arrived in England in 994, the king made no attempt to meet them in battle. According to the Anglo-Saxon Chronicle, 'here Olaf and Swein came to London with ninety-four ships; and determinedly attacked the town, and they also wanted to set it on fire'. The Londoners managed to drive the Vikings away, but they then moved through the country 'and wrought as much harm as any raiding-army ever could, in all things wherever they travelled'. Ethelred and his council again decided on a tribute, paying the increased sum of £16,000. This time, Ethelred also resolved to meet with the leader, King Olaf of Norway, personally, giving hostages to the Vikings so that Olaf would come to him at Andover. This time his policy met with some success, since the Norwegian king promised, truthfully, never to return in hostility, but this failed to solve the problem since there were always other raiders ready for plunder.

Ethelred must have been concerned about the fact that in 991 he had been able to buy the Vikings off with £10,000, but by 994 this figure had increased to £16,000, an enormous amount of money. By paying the Danegeld, Ethelred inadvertently showed the Vikings the wealth of the country and increased their expectations of reward. The Vikings would accept Ethelred's tributes when they were offered, but they always returned in greater numbers and the money paid to them always increased.[20] The Danegeld may, therefore, have bought the king some time in which to repair the country after the raids. It was, however, only a short-term remedy and merely encouraged the Vikings to return again, seeking bigger and bigger payment.

In 997, a new raiding army arrived in the West Country. For Elfrida, who owned lands in the area and had been raised there, this must have been a grave concern. The raiders made their way around Devon, plundering anything they found, as well as moving into Cornwall and Wales. This raid became particularly personal to Elfrida when the

Vikings made their way up the River Tamar and burnt her brother's monastery at Tavistock, which he had worked so long to build.[21] Tavistock was the great symbol of Elfrida's own family's commitment to reform and its devastation was daunting, with the building lying in ruins for several years.

By the late 990s, it must have been clear to everyone in England that the Viking raids were not simply going to go away and that a more concerted policy was required to defeat them. Ethelred was at a loss as to what exactly he should do and, in 1002, he agreed to pay the Vikings £24,000 'on condition they should leave off from their evil deeds'.[22] Once again, this payment shows a huge leap in the amounts that the Vikings expected, and finding the money must have been a source of worry across the kingdom. This payment was followed in 1006 by a further payment of £30,000.[23] Although the Vikings kept on coming, for Ethelred, there must have been some small consolation in the fact that they appeared to be content with raiding and accepting the Danegeld. This changed in 1013, when the purpose of the Viking attacks went suddenly from merely raiding to a campaign of conquest, a disaster for Ethelred and his kingdom that his mother mercifully did not live to see.

Ethelred's entire reign was dominated by the return of the Vikings and it is on his response to these attacks that his reputation principally lies. On her return to court in 993 Elfrida was elderly, although the fact of the Vikings meant that she could not settle down to a comfortable old age.

14

ELFRIDA'S OLD AGE

Elfrida returned to court in the midst of the Viking attacks in 993, escorting her young grandsons.[1] Her return proved permanent, and she attended royal council meetings and took part in lawsuits almost to the end of her life.

Elfrida's reappearance coincided with Ethelred's first charter of restitution made at Pentecost 993.[2] This charter marked the first stage in the reversal of the king's hostile policy towards the Church, with his mother's appearance particularly poignant (and deliberate) given that, by then, she was the last prominent adherent of Edgar's religious reform. The charter dwelt on the fact that the death of Bishop Ethelwold had caused Ethelred to go astray and it was probably deemed apt that the bishop's closest supporter, Elfrida, was present to witness the king's contrition.

After nine years in exile, Elfrida was prepared to accept a slightly lower position than she had previously enjoyed in charter witness lists and, in the first charter of restitution, she witnessed only after the bishops.[3] She was philosophical about this drop in status and at least pleased to see that she was listed as the king's mother, an important recognition of her queenship. She continued to witness after the bishops as the king's mother right up to 999, suggesting she accepted her demotion from the years of Ethelred's minority.[4] She at least witnessed ahead of her grandsons, the Aethelings, showing that her status as a consecrated queen was still considered to be important at court.

In Ethelred's first charter of restitution, Elfrida was immediately followed as a witness by her grandsons, Athelstan, Ecgbert, Edmund and Eadred, suggesting that she brought them to court with her.[5] It was obviously usual for Aelfthryth to attend council meetings in the company of her grandsons and she appears in no surviving charter of the 990s without them, demonstrating her continuing role in their upbringing.[6] The Aethelings also only appear in one charter without their grandmother, suggesting that they were often in each other's company. Given their youth, Elfrida's involvement is no surprise and she must have taken part in the princes' political education. Of all her grandchildren, she may have been closest to her eldest grandson, Athelstan, who remembered her so fondly in his Will. He, like his other brothers, died young. Only Edmund, the third Aetheling, survived to wear the crown, ruling for some months in 1016 following Ethelred's death and, eventually, pragmatically attempting to share the kingdom with the Viking conqueror, Cnut. When Ethelred's descendants eventually returned to the throne in 1042, the king was Edward the Confessor, born after his grandmother's death, although the survival of Edmund's offspring ensures that Elfrida retained a stake in the bloodline of the kings of England and, indeed, Europe. She has many thousands of descendants today.

Elfrida had kept up to date with the politics of England during her exile and slipped easily back into a position of power in the 990s. She was obviously considered an important person in

England, as can be seen in her position as a beneficiary in the Will of a certain Elfflaed, written around 1000 or 1002.[7] In this Will, bequests were made to Ethelred and, also, land at Woodham in Essex was bequested to Elfrida for life, something which suggests that she was influential enough to, potentially, be of use in ensuring that a Will was permitted to stand, even right at the very end of her long life.

Ethelred welcomed his mother back to court, perhaps seeking her advice after his years of poor advisors. He was generous to her in the 990s, something that may have been an attempt to compensate her for her exile, which would almost certainly have involved the confiscation of some of her lands. A grant of land at Brabourne and other estates in Kent in 996 gives some evidence of the respectful and, to some extent, fond relationship Ethelred had with his mother by the late 990s:

[I] have concluded by a grant to my venerable mother, Aelfthryth by name, certain pieces of land in different places, namely seven ploughlands, [three and a half] in the place which is called Brabourne, and three and a half in the same place which is called Evegate, moreover two also in the field of the citizens, and three in addition in the place which the inhabitants are accustomed to call Nachington; and also three at Chalk and one at Wirigens, on condition that she is to have and possess these aforesaid lands as long as she may retain the vital spirit unextinguished in the mortal flesh; and then, indeed, she is to leave it to what heir she pleases in succession to her.[8]

Clearly Ethelred respected his mother and he spoke of her 'vital spirit', reflecting on the keen interest she still showed in the government of the country, in spite of her advanced age. By the late 990s Elfrida was in her late fifties and had already outlived most of her own generation. Both she and her brother, Ordulf, who remained a close advisor to Ethelred up to 1005,[9] must have appeared as relics from the past and, perhaps, an important link with the happier and more peaceful times of King Edgar. Ordulf himself survived his sister, finally dying in around 1008.[10]

For all her advanced age, Elfrida maintained a keen interest in politics and the law until the end of her life, particularly where it enabled her to benefit her kin. She was probably related to a noblewoman called Wynflaed who was involved in a lawsuit with a man called Leofwine. According to the record of the lawsuit, the noblewoman claimed that she had arranged to swap estates with Leofwine and he had later gone back on this deal. Wynflaed was clearly of some consequence and she was able to attract some of the highest members of court to attest as her witness that the transfer actually occurred. The case was heard before the king while his court was at Woolmer and, when Wynflaed was called to present her case, she produced as her witnesses 'Archbishop Sigeric and Bishop Ordbriht and Earl Aelfric and Aelfthryth, the king's mother, all of whom bore witness that Aelfric gave Wynflaed the estates at Hagbourne and at Bradfield in return for the estate at Datchet'.[11] These witnesses would have taken some beating by Leofwine. Elfrida was prepared to appear as a witness and there is evidence that she maintained an interest in the case, seeking to preserve Wynflaed's interests.

On hearing the evidence of the case, Ethelred immediately sent for Leofwine and informed him of Wynflaed's witnesses, expecting him to abandon the case.[12] Leofwine, however, insisted that the matter be referred to a shire meeting and Ethelred, perhaps exasperated, allowed the case to be heard in a meeting at Cuckamsley. Wynflaed, with the help of Elfrida, who shows a strong knowledge of the law, had prepared for the possibility that the matter would be referred to the shire court and, according to the document recording the case,

> Archbishop Sigeric sent his declaration to the meeting and Bishop Ordbriht his. Then Wynflaed was informed that she might prove her ownership of the estate, and she adduced proof of ownership with the help of Aelfthryth, the king's mother.[13]

Just what proof Wynflaed produced is not recorded, but it is clear that the queen played a major role in helping her to secure it. Clearly, Elfrida took a great deal of interest in this case and she probably also helped Wynflaed assemble a number of supporters to attest for her at the shire court since the claimant is recorded as having been supported by a number of women, as well as Elfic, the Aethelings' seneschal.[14] Both Wynflaed and Elfrida must have been pleased when the council, on seeing the strength of Wynflaed's case, ordered Leofwine to hand over the estate and pay compensation. He was also forced to swear that he would make no further claim to the land.

In spite of her advanced age, Elfrida played a major role in the lawsuit between Wynflaed and Leofwine. Her testimony was also sought in a further case that she took a major role in, sometime between 995 and 1002.

During Edgar's reign, Elfrida had played a part in persuading him to renew the freedom of Taunton for the see at Winchester.[15] This was at the behest of Bishop Ethelwold and involved the return of a large estate at Taunton from the Crown to the Church.[16]

Elfrida's own account of what happened next survives, written at some point between 995 and 1002. Given that this is Elfrida's only surviving letter and the only chance to actually hear her own words, quite apart from being the earliest surviving letter of an English queen, it is quoted in full:

Aelfthryth sends humble greetings to Archbishop Aelfric and Earl Aethelweard. I bear witness that Archbishop Dunstan assigned Taunton to Bishop Aethelwold, in conformity with the Bishop's charters. And King Edgar then relinquished it, and commanded every one of his thegns who had any land on the estate that they should hold it in conformity with the bishop's wish, or else give it up. And the king said that he had no land to grant out, when he durst not, for fear of God, retain the headship himself; and moreover he then put Ruishton under the Bishop's control. And then Wulfgyth rode to me at Combe and sought me. And I then, because she was my kinswoman, and Aelfswyth because he [Leofric] was her brother, obtained from Bishop Aethelwold that they [Wulfgyth and Loefric] might enjoy the land for their lifetime, and after their deaths the land should go to Taunton, with produce and with men, just as it stood. And with great difficulty we two brought matters to this conclusion. Now I have been told that Bishop Aethelwold and I must have obtained the title deed by force. Now I, who am alive, am not aware of any force any more than he would be, if he were still alive. For Leofric had a new title deed; when he gave it up he thereby manifested that he would engage in no false dealings in the matter. Then Bishop Aethelwold told him that none of his successors could dispossess him. He then commanded two documents to be written, one he kept himself, the other he gave to Leofric.[17]

Elfrida's words show that, even near the end of her life, her mind remained sharp and her memory good. She recalled the details of a transaction that had occurred around thirty years before and was anxious to exonerate both herself and her old friend, Bishop Ethelwold, from any wrongdoing. The letter, first and foremost, shows a loyalty by Elfrida both towards those who were her kin and towards her old friend. Although a devoted follower of the religious reform, she was not prepared to let these ideals affect the welfare of her kin. According to the letter, Edgar returned the royal lands at Taunton to the church at Winchester and, as a result of this transfer, thegns who had held the land directly from the king now held it from the church.[18] Ethelwold was anxious to acquire the land free of tenants, and the thegns such as Leofric, and his wife Wulfgyth, were required to hand over their land to Winchester soon afterwards.

Elfrida had not been immediately aware of the hardship that this policy would entail for her own kinswoman until she received a visit from Wulfgyth, asking for her help. She immediately offered to help, alongside Elfswith, who was Leofric's sister and evidently influential. The queen, anxious to ensure that her kinswoman did not suffer an injustice, went immediately to Ethelwold and persuaded him to allow Wulfgyth and Leofric to remain on the estate for life. It is interesting that the bishop, who was so eager for the return of all former Church property, was so willing to help Wulfgyth and Leofric and it is probable that this was directly as a result of the queen's pleading. Elfrida's letter demonstrates her fondness for the bishop which is also evident from their close working relationship.

It appears that Leofric had attempted to reclaim the estate in the late 990s and used, as his argument, the claim that the queen and the bishop had forced him to hand over the title deed to his land unjustly. Elfrida was, of course, anxious to clear herself of this charge in her letter and quickly dismissed it. She then turned her attention towards exonerating Ethelwold, expressing sorrow that someone would attempt to blacken the name of a dead man who was unable to defend himself. Elfrida may well have consented to give her personal attention to the matter for the sole purpose of preserving Ethelwold's memory and her letter is a clear testament to the fond memories that she had of the bishop. There is no doubt from the letter that the queen remained grateful to Ethelwold and loyal to him until the end of her life, something that suggests a relationship based on like and respect, rather than mere political expediency.

Even in her old age, Elfrida's character was not free from being slandered. The *Liber Eliensis,* which is a history of the monastery at Ely compiled in the post-Conquest period, includes an extraordinary charge regarding the queen's activities as a widow, blaming her for the murder of Byrhtnoth, the reformed monastery's first abbot, who had been appointed by Bishop Ethelwold himself. According to the *Liber Eliensis,* Byrhtnoth was riding through the New Forest on his way to visit the king's court.

Feeling the urge, he dismounted from his horse and 'sought some more secluded spot to satisfy the needs of nature; as he was a modest man and of great integrity he took care to look round on every side'. He happened to glance under a certain tree where he found Elfrida, whom he recognised, busily preparing a magic potion in order to allow her to transform herself temporarily into horse 'so that she might satisfy the unrestrainable excess of her burning lust, running and leaping hither and thither with horses, and showing herself, shamelessly to them regardless of the fear of

God and the honour of the royal dignity'. Byrhtnoth was very upset at this and withdrew quickly, continuing on his way to court. Once there, protocol meant that the abbot could not be seen to publicly shun King Ethelred's mother and so he went to visit her in her apartments and was, presumably, relieved at finding them empty.

When Elfrida heard of the abbot's arrival, she sent for him immediately, claiming that she wished to discuss the salvation of her soul with him. Byrhtnoth, hoping to reform her, hurried to her apartments and was horrified to find the elderly queen far from penitent. Terrified that the abbot would betray her sorcery and sexual activity to her son, Elfrida appeared before the abbot dressed in all her finery and tried to seduce him in an effort to prevent him from exposing her. The abbot refused her and attempted to make a hasty getaway, intending to go at once to the king. This was something Elfrida, whose return to court had been hard-won, could not allow, and she summoned the women of her household. She then ordered her women to put the abbot to death in a way that would leave no marks on his body. As the queen watched, they heated sword-thongs on the fire before pressing them into Byrhtnoth's bowels until he died. The women then began to cry out until others rushed in to find the abbot dead. Believing the death to be of natural causes, the monks returned the body to Ely, while Elfrida concealed her crime until she herself confessed to it much later, in a fit of remorse.

The *Liber Eliensis*'s claims must rank as the most far-fetched of tales to have become attached to Edgar's queen. While, given her association with Wherwell, the New Forest is a probable location for Elfrida, nothing else about the story rings true. Byrhtnoth did not die until 996–9 and the idea that he was murdered by a lust-filled queen mother is laughable. In reality, this is yet another way in which Elfrida's reputation has been distorted in the religious houses, perhaps as a result of her attempts to interfere in them. Witchcraft was a serious charge in Anglo-Saxon England and there is no contemporary hint that the queen was suspected of practising sorcery. Similarly, the idea of the elderly queen, who by that stage was living in semi-retirement at Wherwell nunnery, going out into the forest every now and again to transform herself into a horse is ridiculous.

It was not unusual for elderly widowed queens to take holy orders or, at least, spend time in a religious community, something that is likely to have appealed to Elfrida given her religious views. During her old age, she continued to show an interest in the nunneries, as exhorted to in the *Regularis Concordia* and, in around 993, she came into direct conflict with Wulfhild, Edgar's former chosen bride. According to the Life of St Wulfhild, written in the late eleventh century by Goscelin of Saint-Bertin, Elfrida took an unwelcome interest in the nunnery, after being exhorted by some members of the community at Barking to expel Abbes Wulfhild in exchange for money.[19] Using her power under the *Regularis Concordia*, Elfrida ordered that Wulfhild be stripped of her position and forced to leave the nunnery.[20] According to the Life, when Wulfhild prepared to leave, her nuns 'accompanied the sweet mother as she left, like a funeral column of weeping daughters, as if wishing to accompany her on her exile'.[21] The abbess, undaunted, declared that she would go to Barking's sister house at Horton, but that she would return in twenty years time to rule as abbess over them once more.

The Life obviously presents a very favourable picture of Wulfhild but an analysis of the source suggests divisions in the house, and that Elfrida might have acted in an attempt to reform the house, as she had promised to do as queen. Certainly, it appears that she took a personal interest in the house, staying there to ensure that her new regime was fully implemented. Personal rivalry with Wulfhild and her kinswoman, Wulfthryth, may also have played a part.

Elfrida found herself dogged with ill luck during her time at Barking, including the mysterious death of all her cattle there and the death of her followers.[22] Finally, when struck down with an illness herself, she gave in and, according to the Life, allowed a jubilant Wulfhild to return to her nunnery. This account is very skewed against Elfrida, but it does show that she could be as hands-on in her zeal for reform as Bishop Ethelwold. The disasters that befell her may perhaps have been sabotage and it does appear that she was made singularly unwelcome at Barking.

There may be some truth in Goscelin's claim that Elfrida 'treated the convent as if her own property', something that would be expected under the terms of the *Regularis Concordia*.[23] She also controlled her nunnery at Wherwell, spending increasing periods of time there as she aged. William of Malmesbury, writing in the twelfth century, commented of Elfrida's retirement,

> Since a mind unregulated is a torment to itself, and a restless spirit endures its own peculiar punishment in this life, Elfrida declining from her regal pride, became extremely penitent; so that at Wherwell, for many years, she clothed her pampered body in hair-cloth, slept at night upon the ground without a pillow, and mortified her flesh with every kind of penance. She was a beautiful woman, singularly faithful to her husband, but deserving punishment from the commission of so great a crime.[24]

The idea that Elfrida went to Wherwell to atone for the death of Edward the Martyr was widespread in the later medieval period, but is probably a misinterpretation of the queen's increasing attempts as she aged to follow something of a religious rule and ascetic life, as Bishop Ethelwold and others that she had known had done before her.

It is generally held that Elfrida caused the growing cult around Edward the Martyr to be suppressed during her lifetime, something which attests to her considerable power at court, although not in relation to the thoughts of the public at large. A lack of official support did not slow down the adoption of Edward's cult, and both Elfrida and Ethelred, who were uncomfortably aware of the criticism directed at them for failing to punish the murderers, had no wish for Ethelred to also be compared to a saintly brother.

In spite of Elfrida's attempts to suppress the cult, Edward was popularly venerated as a saint soon after his murder. The E version of the Anglo-Saxon Chronicle refers to Edward as 'a heavenly saint'.[25] He was also commonly described as a martyr soon after his death, and it is clear from the reports of miracles around his tomb that his sanctity was accepted early. It has also been suggested that Ethelred was more willing than Elfrida to promote the cult of his half-brother during his mother's lifetime since, as a child at the time of the murder, he was in no way to blame for any of the events.[26] There is some evidence that Ethelred took tentative steps towards promoting the cult in the 990s, including establishing a monastery at Cholsey in Berkshire in Edward's honour.[27] The estate on which the monastery was founded had been given to Ethelred by Elfrida, and it is possible that this was another attempt to appease Edward's supporters, as his ceremonial reburial at Shaftesbury had been.

Around 1001, and probably after Elfrida's death, Ethelred finally gave in to popular demand. In a charter granting land at Bradford upon Avon to Shaftesbury Abbey he named his dead brother as both a saint and martyr.[28] This grant was also made expressly to the nuns to provide for Edward's remains and it was the first true official recognition of the dead king as a saint. It is probably no coincidence that his first son born after Elfrida's death was named Edward.[29]

In 1008, Ethelred also took the final step in acknowledging his brother as a saint and ordered that his brother's anniversary be celebrated as a saint's day,[30] Elfrida, whose own supporters had carried out the murder, meaning that she could never punish them, always maintained her policy of suppressing publicity surrounding Edward and his death. It is a testament to her continuing control over Ethelred that she was, largely, able to ensure that he continued in this approach until her death, in spite of his obvious feelings to the contrary.

Elfrida ceased to attest charters in 999, suggesting that this was the date of her final immurement at Wherwell. If she still left the convent, she may also have visited her grandchildren at Dean in Sussex. If this was the case, it is just possible that she was part of one last event in an eventful life. According to the Anglo-Saxon Chronicle for 1001,

> here in this year there was great hostility in the land of the English race through the raiding ship-army; and they raided and burned almost everywhere, so that in a single journey they moved up until they came to Aetheling's Valley [Dean in Sussex]. And then Hampshire came against them there and fought with them. And there Aethelweard, the king's high-reeve, was killed, and Leofric of Whitchurch and Leofwine, the king's high-reeve, and Wulfhere, the bishop's thegn, and Godwine of Worthy, the son of Bishop Aelfsige, and eighty-one men in all. And there were many more of the Danish killed, though they had possession of the place of slaughter.[31]

If Elfrida was still living in 1001 then news of the attack on her former home must have been a terrible shock. It is perhaps fitting that recorded incidents for her long life end with the Vikings, who dogged the reign of her child. The end for Elfrida probably came while she was at Wherwell and attended by the nuns. She died on 17 November.[32] The year is not accurately recorded and it was 1000, 1001 or possibly even 1002. Before 1001 is more likely, given Ethelred's recognition of the cult of Edward the Martyr in that year. She was most likely buried at Wherwell; knowledge of her tomb was forgotten in the later medieval period when her nunnery ceased even to celebrate her *obit* in its calendar of devotions.

Elfrida enjoyed a long life and outlived most of her generation. She did not live to see all the disasters that befell her son, with Ethelred actually fleeing his kingdom in 1013 at an invasion of the Viking king, Sweyn. With Sweyn's death the following year, Ethelred was able to return, but he died in 1016 beset by the attacks of Sweyn's son, Cnut, King of Denmark. Cnut went so far as to marry Ethelred's widow, Emma of Normandy, and although the way was eventually cleared for the accession of Elfrida's grandson, Edward the Confessor, in 1042, the golden age of Anglo-Saxon England had died with King Edgar.

Elfrida, the last of her generation, would have wanted to be remembered as a great reforming queen. Sadly, as a political figure, she stepped on too many toes, especially with regard to the nunneries. For Elfrida, the first woman to be crowned as Queen of England, her reputation will be forever scarred with the death of Edward the Martyr, a crime that the evidence suggests she did not commit. It is time for the real Elfrida, crowned queen, ruler and religious reformer, to step out from the shadows.

NOTES

1 Elfrida's Early Life

1. Searle 1897, pp. 23–4.
2. Finberg 1943, p. 190.
3. Barlow 2003, p. 3.
4. Gaimar, pp. 114–5.
5. William of Worcester, p. 481.
6. Gaimar, p. 115.
7. *Ibid.*, p. 114.
8. *Ibid.*, p. 115.
9. Finberg (1943, p. 197) considers that the missal refers to Ordgar II. Radford (1914, p. 121) thought it was Ordgar I.
10. Many families claimed descent from Ethelred I. For example, a convincing genealogy going back to this king has been assembled for the eleventh-century nobleman Godwin (Anscombe 1913).
11. Finberg 1943, p. 191.
12. Hooke 1994, Bodmin Gospel Manumission f. 89.
13. Ethelred's foundation charter for Tavistock Abbey (Radford 1914, p. 123).
14. Bucknill (2003, p. 41) points out that in one place this 'Alfred' is given a feminine proposition in the document, for example.
15. Finberg 1943, p. 196.
16. *Ibid.*, p. 197.
17. Gaimar, p. 115.
18. *Ibid.*, p. 117.

19. Notices of Tavistock and its Abbey, p. 116.

20. Leofric Missal, f8b.

21. Leofric Missal, plix.

22. The Will of Wynflaed (Whitelock 1930, no. III).

23. The Will of Leofgifu (Whitelock 1930, no. XXIX).

24. Hooke 1994, 7, Manumission from the Bodmin Gospels f. 89.

25. Gaimar, p. 117.

26. Gaimar (p. 117) considered Elfrida to be in possession of an 'honour', which, in this sense, means inheritance. It was in fact given to her on her first marriage as a dowry (Gaimar, p. 119). Examples of women being bequeathed booklands include the ninth-century Earl Alfred's Will in which his daughter, the only child of his second marriage, was well provided for (Harmer 1914, no. X).

27. William of Worcester, p. 479.

28. Yorke 1995, p. 221.

29. Finberg 1946, p. 192.

30. Asser, Chapter 75, pp. 90–91.

31. In the Anglo-Saxon period the role of butler was a noble role rather than that of a servant.

32. Asser, Chapter 23, p. 75.

33. Barlow 2002, p. 33.

34. William of Malmesbury, ii 197 (Mynors 1998, p. 353).

35. Gaimar, p. 120.

36. *Ibid.*, p. 115.

37. *Ibid.*, p. 117.

38. William of Malmesbury (Preest 2002, p. 135).

39. Radford 1914, p. 152.

40. *Ibid.*, p. 152.

41. Finberg 1943, p. 197. Obviously the evidence provided by the thigh bones is rather circular. They are thought to be Ordulf and Ordgar II because Ordulf was known to be tall. Their use as evidence that Ordulf and his descendants were tall should therefore be treated with caution. Another point is that there is no evidence that Elfrida's son, Ethelred, was tall, although he may have taken after his father who is recorded as having been a small man.

42. Finberg 1943, p. 197.

43. *Liber Eliensis*, p. 56.

2 First Marriage

1. Fell 1984, p. 39.

2. Fell 1984, p. 57.
3. Life of St Oswald iii.14.
4. Hart 1973, p. 16.
5. Life of St Oswald iii.14.
6. Hart 1973, p. 118.
7. Will of Ealdorman Ethelwold (Harmer 1914, document xx).
8. Robertson 1956, no. XXII.
9. Life of St Oswald iii.14.
10. An early example of Ethelwold's signature is in charter V (Napier and Stevenson, p. 10), a grant of land of King Eadwig to Archbishop Oda.
11. Life of St Oswald iii.14.
12. *Ibid.*, iii.14.
13. *Ibid.*, i.13.
14. *Ibid.*, iii.14.
15. *Ibid.*, iii.14.
16. Life of St Ethelflaed, p. 19.
17. *Liber Eliensis*, p. 103.
18. Hart 1973, p. 130.
19. Bishop Sideman was appointed Bishop of Crediton in 973, serving until his death in 977. Before that he was Abbot of Exeter, where he was presumably located when first appointed as Edward's tutor.
20. Hart 1973, p. 127.
21. *Ibid.*, p. 122.
22. *Ibid.*, p. 129.
23. *Ibid.*, p. 129.
24. Annals of St Bertin for 862 (Nelson 1991, p. 103).
25. Whitelock 1979, p. 593, no. 128.
26. *Ibid.*, p. 596, no. 130.
27. Gaimar, p. 117.
28. William of Malmesbury (Stephenson p. 139–40).
29. The relationship created through Edgar standing as godfather to Elfrida's child. There is no modern English word to describe it.
30. Bell 1926, p. 278.
31. *Ibid.*, p. 280.
32. Life of St Oswald iii.14.
33. Hart 1973, p. 127.
34. Foundation Charter of a monastery at St Neots in Hart 1966, pp. 27–9.
35. *Chronicon Abbatiae Rameseiensis*, p. 61.

36. *Liber Eliensis*, p. 127.
37. *Ibid.*, p. 127.
38. Yorke 2008, p. 145.
39. Liveing 1906, p. 16.
40. Life of St Ethelflaed of Romsey, p. 19.
41. Liveing 1906, p. 17.
42. Life of St Ethelflaed of Romsey, p. 19.
43. Keynes 2008, p. 28.
44. Knowles *et al.* 2004 for Romsey.
45. Life of St Ethelflaed of Romsey, p. 21.
46. *Ibid.*, p. 20.
47. *Ibid.*, p. 20.
48. *Ibid.*, p. 20.
49. *Ibid.*, p. 23.
50. Yorke 2008, p. 154.
51. Liveing 1906, p. 17.
52. Life of St Oswald, iv.6.
53. Keynes 2008, p. 31.

3 King Edgar

1. William of Malmesbury (Stephenson, p. 129).
2. Aethelweard's Chronicle, p. 54.
3. *Liber Eliensis*, p. 64.
4. Will of Ealdorman Aelfgar (Whitelock 1930, no. II).
5. Ethelflaed's sister, Elfflaed, also left a Will (Whitelock 1930, no. XV).
6. *Liber Eliensis*, p. 64.
7. Ethelflaed's Will (Whitelock 1930, no. XIV).
8. Gaimar, p. 113.
9. The Battle of Brunanburh (in Hamer 1970, p. 43).
10. *Ibid.*
11. ASC E for 946, p. 112.
12. Gaimar, pp. 113–4.
13. Ramsey Chronicle, pp. 11 and p. 52.
14. Hart 1973, p. 124.
15. Yorke 1997, p. 79.
16. *Regularis Concordia* (Symons 1933, p. 1).
17. For example a charter to Archbishop Oda of land at 'Helig' (Crawford Charter V).
18. Aethelweard's Chronicle, p. 55.

19. William of Malmesbury (Stephenson, pp. 138–9).

20. Yorke 2008, p. 146.

21. Aethelweard's Chronicle, p. 55.

22. Aelfric's Life of Dunstan in Whitelock 1979, p. 901.

23. ASC D, p. 113.

24. Statement by Queen Eadgifu about lands in Kent (Hamer 1914, no. xxiii).

25. King Eadred's Will (Hamer 1914, no. xxi).

26. Statement by Queen Eadgifu about land in Kent (Hamer 1914, no. xxiii).

27. Yorke 2008, p. 146.

28. Statement by Queen Eadgifu about land in Kent (Hamer 1914, no. xxiii).

29. For example in an exchange of lands between Brihthelm, Bishp of Wells, and Ethelwold, Abbot of Abingdon is made with Eadwig's permission and witnessed by his wife and her mother (Robertson 1956, no. xxxi).

30. Florence of Worcester, p. 944.

31. Biggs 2008, p. 139.

32. Stafford 1989, p. 49.

33. Gaimar, p. 114.

34. Florence of Worcester, p. 246 and William of Malmesbury (Stephenson, p. 141).

35. Rex 2006, p. 156.

36. Life of St Edith, 3.

37. Wynflaed's Will (Whitelock 1930, no. III).

38. Yorke (2003, p. 83) considers this to be a likely identification.

39. Sydenham 1978, p. 4.

40. *Ibid.*, p. 5.

41. *Ibid.*, p. 8.

42. *Ibid.*, p. 8.

43. Yorke 2003, p. 83.

44. Bucknill 2003, p. 46.

45. Life of St Edith, 2.

46. Hollis 2004a, p. 245.

47. *Ibid.*, p. 250 and Hollis 2004b, p. 305.

48. Life of St Wulfhild, quoted from Hollis 2003c, p. 379.

49. Life of Dunstan (Stubbs, p. 209).

50. William of Malmesbury
(Preest 2002, p. 127).

51. Life of St Edith, 2.

52. William of Malmesbury (Preest 2002, p. 127).
53. Life of St Edith, 5.
54. *Ibid.*, 4.
55. *Ibid.*, 5.
56. William of Malmesbury (Stephenson, p. 141).
57. Gaimar, p. 126.
58. Yorke 2008, p. 150.

4 Elfrida's Marriage and Queenship

1. Gaimar, p. 123.
2. *Ibid.*, p. 124.
3. Bell 1926, p. 282.
4. Gaimar, p. 125.
5. Asser c13.
6. Stafford 2001, p. 56.
7. Pierquin LVI. Yorke (2001, p. 31) advances the argument that Wulfthryth was crowned.
8. Nelson 1986, p. 367.
9. Whitelock 1930, I.
10. *Ibid.*, XI.
11. Robertson, LXIX.
12. Whitelock 1930, IX.
13. *Ibid.*, XXIX.
14. *Liber Eliensis*, p. 128.
15. *Encomium Emmae Reginae,* p. 33.
16. Life of King Edward, p. 42.
17. *Ibid.*, p. 23.
18. Keynes 2008, p. 14.
19. *Ibid.*, p. 10.
20. Whitelock 1930, III.
21. Asser's Life of King Alfred, chapter 13, makes it clear that a king sat on a royal throne and that, if he had a queen, she would sit beside him. An example more contemporary to Elfrida, in the Life of King Edward who Rests at Westminster, chapter VI states that Edith Godwin was also provided with a throne beside the king's.
22. Life of Edith, 12.
23. *Ibid.*, 13.
24. *Ibid.*, 10.
25. *Ibid.*, 4.
26. *Ibid.*, 5.

27. Whitelock 1930, VIII.

28. *Ibid.*, III.

29. Life of King Edward who Rests at Westminster, chapter VI.

30. Life of Edith, 8 and 11.

31. *Ibid.*, 11.

32. *Liber Eliensis* III.50 (Inventory 5 January 1134 of the goods of the church).

33. *Ibid.*, III.122.

34. *Ibid.*, II.50.

35. Life of Edith, 23.

36. *Ibid.*, 11.

37. Orderic Vitallis, Book XI chapter 38.

38. ASC E for 1003.

39. Stafford 2001, p. 110.

40. Whitelock 1930, III.

41. *Ibid.*, XX.

42. Meyer 1993, p. 81.

43. *Ibid.*, p. 90.

44. Statement by Queen Eadgifu about land in Kent (Harmer, XXIII).

45. S1515 (in Sawyer 1968, p. 424).

46. Whitelock 1930, II.

47. *Ibid.*, XIV.

48. Tollerton Hall 2005, p. 141.

49. Whitelock 1930, VIII.

50. Elfgifu mentions land at Hatfield in her Will, as does Ethelflaed of Damerham's sister who noted that the land had been a gift from her sister to the monastery at Stoke (Whitelock 1930, XV). Ethelflaed *Eneda*'s father appears to have held land there according to the *Liber Eliensis*.

51. Meyer 1993, p. 88.

52. S724 (in Sawyer 1968, p. 235).

53. Finberg 1943, p. 190.

54. Gaimar, p. 131.

55. Whitelock 1930, XV.

5 The Tenth-Century Religious Reform

1. Sayles 1948, p. 111.

2. Godfrey 1962, p. 294.

3. *Ibid.*, p. 297.

4. *Ibid.*, p. 297.

5. Sayles 1948, p. 111.

6. Thacker 1997, p. 46.

7. William of Malmesbury (Preest 2002, p. 19).

8. Sayles 1948, p. 113.

9. *Ibid.*, p. 114.

10. An Old English Account of King Edgar's Establishment of the Monasteries (Whitelock 1979, p. 921).

11. *Regularis Concordia.*

12. An Old English Account of King Edgar's Establishment of the Monasteries (Whitelock 1979, p. 921).

13. Sayles 1948, p. 112.

14. *Ibid.*, p. 112.

15. *Ibid.*, p. 112.

16. William of Malmesbury (in Stephenson, p. 129).

17. *Ibid.*, p. 129.

18. *Ibid.*, p. 130.

19. William of Malmesbury (in Preest 2002, p. 19).

20. William of Malmesbury (in Stephenson, p. 131).

21. William of Malmesbury (in Preest 2002, p. 19).

22. Aelfric's Life of St Aethelwold (in Whitelock 1979, p. 904) and Historia Ecclesie Abbendonensis 24.

23. Aelfric's Life of St Aethelwold (in Whitelock 1979, p. 905).

24. William of Malmesbury (in Preest 2002, p. 109).

25. William of Malmesbury (in Preest 2002, p. 110).

26. *Historia Ecclesie Abbendonensis.*

27. Wulfstan of Winchester's Life of Aethelwold (in Lapidge and Winterbottom 1991, pp. 19–21).

28. *Ibid*, p. 21.

29. *Ibid.* p. 21.

30. Yorke 1997b, p. 82.

31. The gifts of Bishop Ethelwold to Peterborough (Robertson, xxxix).

32. ASC E for 96333. Life of St Oswald III.5.

34. Godfrey 1962, p. 304.

35. *Ibid.*, p. 305.

36. Meyer 1993, p. 94.

37. Tavistock is also claimed as his burial place by William of Malmesbury but, since King Ethelred referred to his mother and uncle's graves in Tavistock in its foundation charter but made no mention of his grandfather's, this would seem highly unlikely.

38. William of Malmesbury (in Preest 2002, p. 135).

39. William of Malmesbury (in Preest 2002, p. 136).
40. Finberg 1943, p. 193.

6 Elfrida's Role in the Reform Movement

1. *Liber Eliensis* (Fairweather 2005, p. 135).
2. *Liber Eliensis,* p. 47.
3. ASC E.
4. Aelric's Life of St Aethelwold (in Whitelock 1979, p. 906).
5. Godfrey 1962, p. 302.
6. *Liber Eliensis*, p. 37.
7. *Regularis Concordia*, p. 4.
8. *Ibid.*, p. 2.
9. Heslop 2005, p. 796.
10. Hollis 1992, p. 209.
11. Prescott 2002, p. 5.
12. *Regularis Concordia*, p. 4.
13. *Ibid.*, p. 6.
14. Schulenburg 1989, p. 263.
15. *Ibid.*, p. 275.
16. *Ibid.*, p. 292.
17. Life of Edith, 6 and 7.
18. *Ibid.*, 7.
19. *Ibid.*, 16.
20. *Ibid.*, 14.
21. Hollis 2004a, p. 255.
22. Life of Edith, 11.
23. *Regularis Concordia*, p. 7.
24. *Ibid.*, p. 7.
25. *Ibid.*, p. 16.
26. For example, ASC A (in Swanton 2000, pp. 116–8).
27. William of Malmesbury (in Preest 2002, p. 276).
28. Aelfric's Life of St Aethelwold (in Whitelock 1979, p. 907).
29. *Ibid.*
30. *Ibid.*
31. *Ibid.*
32. Wulfstan of Winchester's Life of Aethelwold (in Lapidge and Winterbottom 1991, p. 37).
33. New Minster Charter in Rumble IV.
34. Godfrey 1962, p. 302.
35. Aelfric's Life of St Aethelwold (in Whitelock 1979, pp. 907–8).

36. William of Malmesbury (in Stephenson, p. 132).
37. Godfrey 1962, p. 304.
38. Simeon of Durham (in Stevenson 1987, p. 92).
39. William of Malmesbury (in Preest 2002, p. 94).
40. *Ibid.*, p. 94.
41. *Ibid.*, p. 276.
42. Yorke 1997a, p. 5.
43. ASC E for 963.
44. Renewal of the freedom of Taunton by King Edgar (in Robertson 1939, p. 93).
45. *Ibid.*, p. 95.
46. Elfrida gives testimony concerning an estate at Ruishton 995–1005 (in Harmer 1952, p. 396).
47. Godfrey 1962, p. 303.
48. Adjustment of the boundaries between the monasteries of Winchester (in Robertson 1939, p. 103).
49. *Ibid.*, p. 103.
50. *Ibid.*, p. 105.

7 Imperial Ambitions

1. New Minster Refoundation Charter (Rumble IV).
2. Stafford 1989, p. 41.
3. Dumville 1976, p. 43.
4. Yorke 1997b, p. 84.
5. Whitelock 1930, IX.
6. William of Malmesbury (in Stephenson, p. 139).
7. William of Malmesbury (in Preest 2002, p. 279).
8. Stenton 1971, p. 368.
9. *Ibid.*, p. 368.
10. Extract from the Ruin (in Hamer 1970, p. 27).
11. Nelson 1986, p. 373.
12. Lavelle 2002, p. 30.
13. Nelson 1986, p. 373.
14. Life of St Oswald IV.6 contains an account of the coronation written by a contemporary. It is heavily based on the coronation ordo and therefore not an eyewitness account as such, although it does give extra details that suggest the author had additional knowledge of what had occurred.
15. ASC E for 972 (really 973).
16. Florence of Worcester (in Stephenson, p. 86).

17. William of Malmesbury (in Stephenson, p. 130).
18. *Ibid.*
19. Stafford 1989, p. 56.
20. Edgar IV Lawcode (in Whitelock 1979, p. 435).
21. *Ibid.* p. 437.
22. Life of St Oswald IV.11.

8 The Heirs of King Edgar

1. Lavelle 2002, p. 34.
2. Stafford 1983, p. 64.
3. ASC D.
4. ASC D.
5. William of Malmesbury (in Stephenson, p. 113).
6. William of Malmesbury (in Stephenson, p. 109).
7. William of Malmesbury (in Stephenson, p. 116).
8. *Encomium Emmae Reginae* (in Campbell 1998, p. 41).
9. Life of St Oswald (in Whitelock 1979, p. 914).
10. Eadmer (in Bosanquet 1964, p. 4).
11. S937.
12. William of Malmesbury (in Stephenson, p. 142).
13. Exchange of lands between Ethelwold, Bishop of Winchester, and Elfwine is witnessed by both Edward the Martyr and Bishop Ethelwold, for example, and the exchange also included the king's consent (Robertson, liii).
14. *Liber Eliensis*, p. 11.
15. Yorke 1997b, p. 85.
16. For example, lease of land by Oswald, Bishop of Worcester to Ethelm (Robertson, xxxiv).
17. ASC D for 975 (in Swanton 2000, p. 121).
18. Fisher 1952, p. 255.
19. Godfrey 1962, p. 307.
20. Life of Oswald IV.12.
21. ASC A for 901 (actually 899).
22. ASC A for 905 (actually 903).
23. The *Encomium Emmae Reginae* merely records that Edmund died (in Campbell 1998, p. 31) but William of Malmesbury claims that he was murdered (in Stevenson 1989, p. 168).
24. *Encomium Emmae Reginae* (in Campbell 1998, p. 45).
25. Life of St Oswald (in Whitelock 1979, p. 912).
26. Simeon of Durham (in Stevenson 1987, p. 94).

27. Godfrey 1962, p. 308.
28. Life of Oswald IV.12.
29. For example, Henry of Huntingdon (in Forrestor 1853, p. 176).
30. William of Malmesbury (in Stephenson, p. 142).
31. *Ibid.*
32. *Ibid.*
33. William of Malmesbury (in Stephenson, p. 143).
34. Williams 2003, p. 11.

9 The Murder of Edward the Martyr

1. Manuscript A was copied *c.* 1001–1013, fixing its date (in Swanton 2000, p. xxii).
2. ASC A for 978.
3. ASC C for 978.
4. ASC E for 979 (actually 978).
5. Swanton 2000, p. xxvi.
6. *Historia Ecclesie Abbendonensis* 95 and B214.
7. Stowell 1970, p. 99.
8. Life of St Oswald (in Whitelock 1979, p. 914).
9. Stowell 1970, p. 102.
10. Stowell 1970, p. 118.
11. The sequence is detailed in Stowell 1970, 117.
12. Life of St Oswald.
13. *Ibid.* 20.
14. Williams 2003, p. 12.
15. Osbern's Life of St Dunstan (in Stubbs 1874, p. 114).
16. Fell 1971, p. xvi.
17. Fell 1971, p. xvi.
18. Fell 1971 contains the text of the *Passion of Edward the Martyr.*
19. Keen 1999, p. 100.
20. Simeon of Durham (in Stevenson 1987, p. 95).
21. Eadmer (in Bosanquet 1964, p. 3), Florence of Worcester (in Stephenson, p. 87).
22. William of Malmesbury (in Stephenson, p. 143).
23. Henry of Huntingdon (in Forrester 1853, p. 177).
24. Gaimar, line 3991.
25. *Ibid.*, line 4004.
26. *Ibid.*, line 4017.
27. *Ibid.*, line 4025.
28. *Ibid.*, line 4030.

29. *Ibid.*, line 4035.

30. *Ibid.*, line 4043.

31. Wright 1939, p. 170.

32. The Sermon of the Wolf (in Whitelock 1979, p. 931).

33. ASC E for 979 (actually 978).

34. Keynes 1980, p. 167.

35. Life of Edith 18.

36. Document 58 in Bucknill 2003, p. 48.

37. Yorke 2008, 154.

10 The Aftermath of the Murder

1. William of Malmesbury (in Stephenson, p. 144).

2. *Ibid.* p. 145.

3. Gaimar, line 4053.

4. Gaimar, line 4075.

5. Life of St Oswald (in Whitelock 1979, p. 915).

6. Sermon of the Wolf (in Whitelock 1979, p. 931).

7. William of Malmesbury (in Preest 2002, p. 124).

8. William of Malmesbury (in Stephenson, p. 123).

9. Wilson-Claridge 1984, p. 2.

10. Life of Edith 19.

11. ASC E for 979 (actually 978).

12. William of Malmesbury (in Stephenson, p. 143).

13. William of Malmesbury (in Preest 2002, p. 125).

14. William of Malmesbury (in Preest 2002, p. 125).

15. ASC E for 980.

16. Wilson-Claridge 1984, p. 2.

17. Dates given by Elizabeth Shelford, the Tudor Abbess of Shaftesbury (Sydenham 1978, p. 8).

18. Life of St Oswald (in Whitelock 1979, p. 915).

19. Life of Edith 18.

20. William of Malmesbury (in Stephenson, p. 145).

21. Florence of Worcester, p. 87.

22. *Ibid.*

23. Life of St Oswald (in Whitelock 1979, p. 916).

24. Eadmer, p. 4.

25. William of Malmesbury (in Stephenson, p. 145).

26. Florence of Worcester, p. 87.

11 Ethelred's Minority

1. Keynes 1980, p. 174.
2. Stenton 1971, p. 405.
3. *Ibid.*
4. Stafford 2001, p. 199.
5. S835, S837, S838, S840, S841, S842, S843, S845, S849, S855.
6. Stevenson 1858, p. 372.
7. Charter 26: King Aethelred confirms the bequest of Aethelmaer Dux of land to St Saviour's Minster in 982, and Charter 27: Aethelred grants Meadowland north of Winchester to Bishop Aethelgar in 983 (in Miller 2001).
8. Lavelle 2002, p. 84.
9. Keynes 1980, p. 157.
10. For example, Ethelwold is the fifth witness, behind Ethelred, Elfrida, Dunstan and Oswald on Charters 26 and 27 of the New Minster (in Miller 2001).
11. Stafford 1989, p. 60.
12. Williams 2003, p. 22.
13. Wulfstan of Winchester's Life of St Aethelwold (in Lapidge and Winterbottom 1991, p. 61).
14. Yorke 1997b, p. 85.
15. Wulfstan of Winchester's Life of St Aethelwold (in Lapidge and Winterbottom 1991, p. 61).
16. Godfrey 1962, p. 308.
17. *Ibid.*
18. Yorke 1997b, p. 85.
19. *Ibid.*
20. It has also been suggested, although on limited evidence, that Elfrida founded two further nunneries at Andover at Reading during Ethelred's minority (Hall 1854, p. 253).
21. Yorke 2003, p. 78.
22. Yorke 2003, p. 99.
23. William of Malmesbury (in Preest 2002, p. 116).
24. William of Malmesbury (in Preest 2002, p. 124).
25. Life of King Edward who Rests at Westminster (in Barlow 1962, p. 47).
26. Stafford 2001, p. 75.
27. Bucknill 2003, p. 56.
28. Life of Edith 23.
29. Goscelin, 'The Translatio of Edith', 7.

30. Aelfric's Life of Aethelwold (in Whitelock 1979, p. 911).
31. *Ibid.*, p. 907.
32. *Ibid.*, p. 909.
33. *Ibid.*
34. Prescott 2002, p. 4.
35. *Ibid.*

12 Elfrida's Obscurity

1. Yorke 1997b, p. 85.
2. ASC D for 1043.
3. ASC E for 1043.
4. ASC E for 1052.
5. Estates known to have belonged to Elfrida are listed in Meyer 1993, pp. 106–13.
6. Keynes 1980, p. 181.
7. Charter S876 (translated by Keynes 1980, p. 176). Original text in Stevenson 1858, p. 360.
8. S876 (in Keynes 1980, p. 177).
9. Barlow 2003, p. 25.
10. *Ibid.*
11. Yorke 1997b, p. 85.
12. ASC E and C for 986.
13. Florence of Worcester (in Stephenson, p. 88).
14. Charters S885 and S893 (Discussed in Keynes 1980, p. 179).
15. Charter S876 (Discussed in Keynes 1980, p. 177).
16. *Ibid.*
17. Charter S891 (Discussed in Keynes 1980, p. 180).
18. Charter 28 (in Miller 2001, pp. 134–5).
19. Simeon of Durham (in Stevenson 1987, p. 96).
20. Williams 2003, p. 24.
21. *Ibid.*
22. *Ibid.*
23. Stafford 2001, p. 85 and Williams 2003, p. 25.
24. Stafford 1997, p. 66.
25. Williams 2003, p. 28.
26. Old English Will of the Aetheling Athelstan, Eldest Son of King Aethelred (Whitelock 1930, xx).
27. S1503 and S904, both refer to Aelfthryth's use of the land.
28. Aetheling Athelstan's Will.
29. Williams 2003, p. 29.

13 The Return of the Vikings

1. ASC C for 980.
2. ASC C for 981.
3. ASC C for 982.
4. ASC A for 866 (actually 865).
5. ASC A for 993 (actually 991).
6. *Encomium Emmae Reginae* (in Campbell 1998, pp. 19–21).
7. *Encomium Emmae Reginae* (in Campbell 1998, p. 23).
8. William of Malmesbury (in Preest 2002, p. 279).
9. William of Malmesbury (in Preest 2002, p. 280).
10. Stenton 1971, p. 376.
11. Lavelle 2002, p. 67.
12. Stenton 1971, p. 376.
13. The Battle of Maldon (in Hamer 1970, p. 59).
14. The Battle of Maldon (in Hamer 1970, p. 53).
15. Stenton 1971, p. 377.
16. Asser chapter 20 (in Keynes and Lapidge 2004, p. 74).
17. William of Malmesbury (in Stephenson, p. 146).
18. Simeon of Durham (in Stevenson 1987, p. 96).
19. Anglo-Saxon Chronicle F for 992 (in Swanton 2000, p. 126).
20. Eadmer (in Bosanquet 1964, p. 4).
21. ASC F for 997.
22. ASC E for 1002.
23. ASC E for 1006.

14 Elfrida's Old Age

1. Elfrida witnesses several charters between 993 and 999 (in Keynes 1980, p. 176).
2. Charter S876 (in Stevenson 1858, p. 365).
3. *Ibid.*
4. Charter of 999 giving land at Huredes (in Stevenson 1858, p. 376).
5. Charter S876 (in Stevenson 1858, p. 365).
6. Stafford 2001, p. 199.
7. S1486 (in Sawyer 1968, p. 415).
8. Grant by Aethelred to his mother of Brabourne and other estates in Kent (996) (in Whitelock 1979, pp. 575–6).
9. Finberg 1943, p. 193.
10. *Ibid.*
11. S1454 Record of a Lawsuit between Wynflaed and Leofwine (in

Robertson 1939, p. 137).

12. *Ibid.*

13. *Ibid.*

14. *Ibid.*

15. Renewal of the Freedom of Taunton by King Edgar (in Robertson 1939, p. 39).

16. Harmer 1952, p. 380.

17. Aelfthryth gives testimony concerning an estate at Ruishton 995–1002 (in Harmer 1952, pp. 396–7).

18. Harmer 1952, p. 380.

19. *La Vie de Sainte Vulfhilde par Goscelin de* Cantorbery, Analecta Bollandiana 32 (1913), pp. 10–26.

20. *Ibid.*

21. *Ibid.*

22. *Ibid.*

23. *Ibid.*

24. William of Malmesbury (Stephenson, p. 144).

25. ASC E for 979 (actually 978).

26. Williams 2003, p. 17.

27. Williams 2003, p. 14.

28. S899 King Aethelred to Shaftesbury Abbey of Land at Bradford Upon Avon (in Sawyer 1968, pp. 274–5).

29. Lavelle 2002, p. 87.

30. Fell 1971, p. xxi.

31. ASC A for 1001.

32. Stafford 2001, p. 209.

BIBLIOGRAPHY

Place of publication is London unless otherwise stated.

Primary Sources

Barlow, F. (ed.), *The Life of King Edward who Rests at Westminster* (1962).

Blake, E. O. (ed.), *Liber Eliensis* (1962).

Byrhtferth of Ramsey, *The Lives of St Oswald and St Ecgwine*, ed. M. Lapidge (Oxford, 2009).

Campbell, A. (ed.), *The Chronicle of Aethelweard* (1962).

Campbell, A. (ed.), *Encomium Emmae Reginae* (Cambridge, 1998).

Chibnall, M. (ed. and trans.), *The Ecclesiastical History of Orderic Vitalis, Vol VI* (Oxford, 1978).

Eadmer, *Eadmer's History of Recent Events in England*, ed. G. Bosanquet (1964).

Fairweather, J., *Liber Eliensis* (Woodbridge, 2005).

Fell, C. (ed.), *Edward King and Martyr* (Leeds, 1971).

Forester, T., *The Chronicle of Henry of Huntingdon* (1853).

Gaimar, G., *Lestoirie des Engles*, eds T. D. Hardy and C. T. Martin, (1889).

Goscelin of Saint-Bertin, 'The Life of Edith' (trans. M. Wright) and 'The Translatio of Edith' in S. Hollis (ed.), *Writing the Wilton Women* (Turnhout, 2004).

Goscelin of Saint-Bertin, 'La Vie de Sainte Vulfhilde Par Goscelin de Cantorbery' *Analecta Bollandiana*, 32 (1913), pp. 10–26.

Hamer, R. (ed.), *A Choice of Anglo-Saxon Verse* (1970).

Harmer, F. E. (ed.), *Select English Histotical Documents of the Ninth and Tenth Centuries* (Cambridge, 1914).

Hart, C. R., *The Early Charters of Eastern England* (Leicester, 1966).

Hooke, D., *Pre-Conquest Charter-Bounds of Devon and Cornwall* (Woodbridge, 1994).

Hudson, J. (ed.), *Historia Ecclesie Abbendonensis: The History of the Church of Abingdon*, 2 vols (Oxford, 2007).

Keynes, S., *The Diplomas of King Aethelred 'The Unready' 978-1016* (Cambridge, 1980).

Keynes, S. and M. Lapidge (eds), 'Asser's Life of King Alfred', in *Asser's Life of King Alfred and Other Contemporary Sources* (2004).

Lapidge, M. and M. Winterbottom (eds), *Wulfstan of Winchester: The Life of St Aethelwold* (Oxford, 1991).

Liveing, H. G. D., 'Life of St Ethelflaed of Romsey' in *Records of Romsey Abbey* (Winchester, 1906).

Macray, W. D. (ed.), *Chronicon Abbatiae Rameseiensis* (1886).

Miller, S., (ed.), *Charters of the New Minster, Winchester* (Oxford, 2001).

Napier, A. S. and W. H. Stevenson (eds), *The Crawford Collection of Early Charters and Documents* (Oxford, 1895).

Nelson, J. L. (ed.), *The Annals of St Bertin* (Manchester, 1991).

Pierquin, H., *Recueil General Des Chartes Angol-Saxonnes 604–1061* (Paris, 1912).

Preest, D. (ed.), *William of Malmesbury: The Deeds of the Bishops of England* (Woodbridge, 2002).

Prescott, A. (ed.), *The Benedictional of St Aethelwold: A Facsimile* (2002).

Robertson, A. J. (ed.), *Anglo-Saxon Charters* (Cambridge, 1956).

Rumble, A. R. (ed.), *Property and Piety in Early Medieval Winchester* (Oxford, 2002).

Sawyer, P. H., *Anglo-Saxon Charters* (1968).

Stephenson, J. (ed.), *William of Malmesbury: The Kings Before the Conquest (c. 1865)*.

Stevenson, J. (ed.), *Florence of Worcester* (1853).

Stevenson, J. (ed.), *Chronicon Monasterii de Abingdon*, Vol. I (1858).

Stevenson, J. (ed.), *Simeon of Durham: A History of the Kings of England* (1987).

Stubbs, W., *Memorials of St Dunstan* (1874).

Swanton, M. (ed. and trans.), *The Anglo-Saxon Chr*, (2000).

Symons, D. T. (ed.), *Regularis Concordia: The Monastic Agreen. of Monks and Nuns of the English Nation* (1953).

Warren, F. E. (ed.), *The Leofric Missal as used in the Cathedral o, Exeter During the Episcopate of its First Bishop AD 1050–1072* (Oxford, 1883).

Whitelock, D. (ed.), *Anglo-Saxon Wills* (Cambridge, 1930).

Whitelock, D. (ed.), *English Historical Documents* (1979).

Worth, R. N. (ed.), 'William of Worcester: Devon's Earliest Topographer', *Report and Transactions of the Devonshire Association*, 18 (1886).

Secondary Sources

Anscombe, A., 'The Pedigree of Earl Godwin', *Transactions of the Royal Historical Society, Third Series*, vol. 7 (1913).

Barlow, F., *The Godwins* (2003).

Bell, A., 'Gaimar and the Edgar-Aelfthryth Story', *The Modern Language Review*, 21 (1926).

Biggs, F. M., 'Edgar's Path to the Throne' in D. Scragg (ed.), *Edgar, King of the English 959–975* (Woodbridge, 2008).

Dumville, D., 'The Anglian Collection of Royal Genealogies and Regnal Lists', *Anglo-Saxon England*, 5 (1976), pp. 23–50.

Fell, C., *Women in Anglo-Saxon England* (1984).

Finberg, H. P. R., 'The House of Ordgar and the Foundation of Tavistock Abbey', *The English Historical Review*, 58 (1943).

Fisher, D. J. V., 'The Anti-Monastic Reaction in the Reign of Edward the Martyr', *Cambridge Historical Journal*, 10 (1952).

Godfrey, J., *The Church in Anglo-Saxon England* (Cambridge, 1962).

Hall, Mrs M., *The Queens Before the Conquest*, vol. 2 (1854).

Hart, C., 'Athelstan "Half King" and his Family', *Anglo-Saxon England*, vol. 2 (1973).

Heslop, T. A., 'The English Origins of the Coronation of the Virgin', *The Burlington Magazine*, 147 (2005).

Hollis, S., *Anglo-Saxon Women and the Church* (Woodbridge, 1992).

Hollis, S., 'St Edith and the Wilton Community' in S. Hollis (ed.), *Writing the Wilton Women* (Turnhout, 2004a).

Elfrida

...mplative and Bride of Christ' in S. Hollis ...*omen* (Turnhout, 2004b).

... of Learning' Community' in S. Hollis ...*omen* (Turnhout, 2004c).

... *the Early History of Shaftesbury Abbey*

...gar, Rex Admirabilis' in D. Scragg (ed.), *Edgar, King ...glish 959–975* (Woodbridge, 2008).

...ies, D., C. N. L. Brooke and V. C. M. London, *The Heads ...f Religious Houses: England and Wales, 940–1216* (Cambridge, 2004).

Lavelle, R., *Aethelred II: King of the English 978–1916* (Stroud, 2002).

Liveing, H. G. D., *Records of Romsey Abbey* (Winchester, 1906).

Meyer, M. A., 'The Queen's "Demesne" in Later Anglo-Saxon England' in M. A. Meyer (ed.), *The Culture of Christendom* (1993).

Nelson, J. L., *Politics and Ritual in Early Medieval Europe* (1986).

'Notices of Tavistock and its Abbey', *The Gentleman's Magazine*, 147 (1830).

Parsons (ed.), *Medieval Queenship* (Stroud, 1998).

Radford, Mrs G. H., 'Tavistock Abbey', *Report and Transactions of the Devonshire Association*, 46 (1914).

Rex, P., *Edgar, King of the English 959–975* (Stroud, 2007).

Sayles, G. O., *The Medieval Foundations of England* (1948).

Schulenburg, J. T., 'Women's Monastic Communities, 500–1100: Patterns of Expansion and Decline', *Signs*, 14 (1989).

Searle, W. G., *Onomasticon Anglo-Saxonicum: A List of Anglo-Saxon Proper Names From the Time of Beda to that of King John* (Cambridge, 1897).

Stafford, P., *Queens, Concubines and Dowagers* (1983).

Stafford, P., *Unification and Conquest* (1989).

Stafford, P., 'The Portrayal of Royal Women in England, Mid-Tenth to Mid-Twelfth Centuries', in J. C. Parsons (ed.), *Medieval Queenship* (Stroud, 1993).

Stafford, P., *Queen Emma and Queen Edith* (Oxford, 2001).

Stenton, F., *Anglo-Saxon England* (Oxford, 1971).

Stowell, T. E. A., 'The Bones of Edward the Martyr', *The Criminologist*, 5 (1970), pp. 16–17.

Sydenham, L., *Shaftesbury and its Abbey* (1978).

Thacker, A., 'Aethelwold and Abingdon' in B. Yorke (ed.,
Aethelwold: His Career and Influence (Woodbridge, 1997)

Williams, A., *Aethelred the Unready: The Ill-Counselled*
(2003).

Wilson-Claridge, J., *The Recorded Miracles of St Edward Martyr* (1984).

Wormald, P., *The Making of English Law: King Alfred to the Twelfth Century* (Oxford, 1999).

Wright, C. E., *The Cultivation of Saga in Anglo-Saxon England* (Edinburgh, 1939).

Yorke, B., *Wessex in the Early Middle Ages* (1995).

Yorke, B., 'Introduction' in B. Yorke (ed.), *Bishop Aethelwold: His Career and Influence* (Woodbridge, 1997a).

Yorke, B., 'Aethelwold and the Politics of the Tenth Century', in B. Yorke (ed.), *Bishop Aethelwold: His Career and Influence* (Woodbridge, 1997b).

Yorke, B., *Nunneries and the Anglo-Saxon Royal Houses* (2003).

Yorke, B., 'The Women in Edgar's Life' in D. Scragg (ed.), *Edgar, King of the English 959–975* (Woodbridge, 2008).

Unpublished PhD Theses

Bucknill, R. P., *Wherwell Abbey and its Cartulary* (King's College London, 2003).

Tollerton Hall, L., *Wills and Will-Making in Late Anglo-Saxon England* (University of York, 2005).

INDEX

Also available from Amberley Publishing

The Tudor femmes fatales
who changed English history

B

The
Boleyn
Women

ELIZABETH
NORTON

Also available as an ebook
Available from all good bookshops or to order direct
Please call **01453-847-800**
www.amberleybooks.com

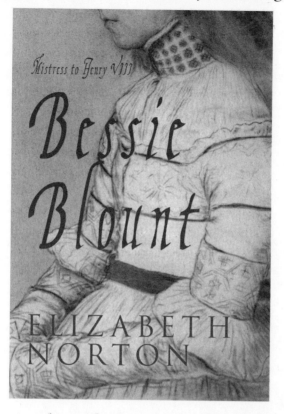

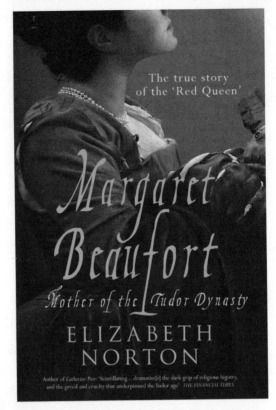